Maria
I wish you
Peace
Susan Brunell

The Dragonfly Spirit

A mother's journey of learning about death, life, and the road back to Peace.

Susan Brunell

authorHOUSE®

AuthorHouse™
1663 Liberty Drive
Bloomington, IN 47403
www.authorhouse.com
Phone: 1 (800) 839-8640

Published by AuthorHouse 01/11/2018

ISBN: 978-1-5462-2273-6 (sc)
ISBN: 978-1-5462-2271-2 (hc)
ISBN: 978-1-5462-2272-9 (e)

Library of Congress Control Number: 2017919661

Print information available on the last page.

This book is printed on acid-free paper.

Contents

Part III

Life After Death

Dedication

This book is dedicated to my best friend, the love of my life and soul mate, my husband, Stephen.

It is also dedicated to my daughters, Sarah and Megan, and my grandson, Alex. You give me a reason to persevere.

The Dragonfly

Once, in a little pond, in the muddy water under the lily pads, there lived a little water beetle in a community of water beetles. They lived a simple and comfortable life in the pond with few disturbances and interruptions.

Once in a while, sadness would come to the community when one of their fellow beetles would climb the stem of a lily pad and would never be seen again. They knew when this happened; their friend was dead, gone forever.

Then, one day, one little water beetle felt an irresistible urge to climb up that stem. However, he was determined that he would not leave forever. He would come back and tell his friends what he had found at the top.

When he reached the top and climbed out of the water onto the surface of the lily pad, he was so tired, and the sun felt so warm, that he decided he must take a nap. As he slept, his body changed and when he woke up, he had turned into a beautiful blue-tailed dragonfly with broad wings and a slender body designed for flying.

So, fly he did! And, as he soared he saw the beauty of a whole new world and a far superior way of life to what he had never known existed.

Then he remembered his beetle friends and how they were thinking by now he was dead. He wanted to go back to tell them, and explain to them that he was now more alive than he had ever been before. His life had been fulfilled rather than ended.

But, his new body would not go down into the water. He could not get back to tell his friends the good news. Then he understood that their time would come, when they, too, would know what he now knew. So, he raised his wings and flew off into his joyous new life!

~Author Unknown~

Introduction

I was told once that when you lose a parent you become an orphan; when you lose your spouse you become a widow, but when you lose a child there is no word for it because it is that horrible. It's true; there is no word for it, and yes, it is that horrible. That is not to say that the other two kinds of grief are not bad, they are also terrible. I sympathize with people experiencing all types of grief.

When people ask me how many children I have my answer is two. My older daughter, Sarah, lives here on Earth, and my younger daughter, Megan, lives in Heaven. It took several years after Megan crossed over for me to be able to say that.

They say that if you are going to write, you should write about what you know. I know that everything in this book is true because I have lived it. It began as a journal of events and progressed to stories. As I combined the stories, a book began to emerge. Some stories may seem difficult to believe, but they are true. It may require an open mind to accept them.

This is a story about learning to grow and cope despite great loss. I hope as you read these pages you will find help dealing with your own losses. I don't pretend to be an expert, and I certainly do not have all of the answers. I don't believe anyone has all of the answers because it is different for each person along this journey, and the thing that helps one may hurt another. I hope you will find ways in this book to work through grief and find peace once again. I also hope to help those who love someone experiencing great loss and grief. Sometimes the things we think will comfort another, only serve to hurt them more. I offer tools to understand the process and be a better support for your loved ones by exposing some of the ways we are hurt during grief. I hope to help heal instead.

This is not a story about death. It's about understanding death. It's about a journey that no parent chooses to take. It's about learning to live life to its fullest in spite of death.

Part I

Learning and Growing

Memories

I remember when I was a freshman in college in 1972 taking English Literature 101. We were assigned to read portions of the book, *Speak, Memory* by Vladamir Nabokov. In the book, Nabokov writes about many details that he recalls from his childhood. I honestly do not remember much of the book, but I do remember an assignment we were given. We were told to think back on the earliest memory from our childhood that we could possibly recall and write an essay about it. The professor said that most people if they really try, will recall something from their third year. The first memory that we have is usually something that has had or will have, an impact on our lives.

I spent a lot of time trying to recall my earliest memory. My mother had three children in her first marriage. Two sons had died as babies. My sister, Barbara, was also from her first marriage. Barbara was seven years old when my mother and father married in 1948 in Las Vegas. My brother Eddy and I were born in Burbank, CA, and we lived in Peco Rivera when I was little. I knew that we had two Boston Terriers. The male was named Pal Boy and the female was named Ginger. Pal Boy was a traditional black and white dog, but Ginger was light brown and, as her name would indicate, she had ginger tones in her coat. I never really remember playing with Ginger, but I had seen pictures of her and my parents had told me stories about her.

As I searched my memory I remembered standing in the yard with my father. He had stooped down close to the ground to speak to me and looked directly into my eyes. Maybe the deliberateness in the way he spoke to me that day is part of the reason I remember it. He told me that I would never see Ginger again; that she had died. I had never heard the word before then. I asked where she was. I remember him telling me that she had stopped breathing; she had gone down into the ground and a special part of her had gone up to Heaven to be with God. He said that she would be safe there and would always be happy. I remember feeling sad, but happy at the same time.

I spoke with my parents about the assignment I was working on and asked them how old I was at the time. They were shocked that I remembered Ginger dying. Then they told me that I was three years old. We were still living in California when she died and moved to New England toward the end of my third year.

As I traveled through my life there were many deaths and subsequent funerals that I remember impacting me and shaping my perception of death, as we all do. My mother was one of eight girls and my father was one of eleven siblings. When I count aunts and uncles and their spouses the number was about thirty-four. I can't even begin to count the number of cousins I ended up with. We don't always think about it, but the bigger the family, and the more friends we have, the more deaths we experience. It's only natural. In some way, we may become immune to the pain of some of the losses. We see it as a part of life, and that is the right way to look at death. At other times the occurrence of death has a profound impact on how we view our world.

As I look back on some of the deaths I have experienced I can see the knowledge and growth I experienced through them.

Grandpa

After we moved to New England I lived in a two-story house that my parents rented. I remember going to visit my Grandpa and Grandma (my mother's parents) in the apartment they lived in at the time. It was on the second floor of a large building on the corner of Main Street, called the Maci Building. My Grandpa used to sit in a rocking chair in the front window. Every day at 6:00 P.M. the fire whistle would blow. I remember sitting on his lap and he would tell me that he had a secret button under the windowsill. He said that he would push that button every day and make the fire whistle blow to let everyone in town know the correct time. I felt amazed by that and thought that he must be the most important person in town.

Grampa died when I was five years old. It was the first funeral I ever attended. My mother and her seven sisters were crying at the funeral. I wasn't sure why they were so sad because to me it just meant that Grandpa was going to go in the ground and then up to Heaven to be with God. Wasn't that a good thing? I remember going up to one of my aunts and telling her to stop crying because she would see Grandpa again when she went to Heaven. I couldn't understand why she cried even harder after that, I thought to hear that would make her happy.

A short time after Grandpa died I started to become aware of a feeling at night after I would get into bed. It felt like Grandpa was in my room, standing in the corner. Like he wanted to say something to me, but couldn't. I found it very comforting, and I wanted to talk with him. I told him that I missed him and loved him. I told him that I knew he was okay because the fire whistle still blew every day at 6:00 P.M. When I told my mother that Grandpa came to be with me at night she asked me if I was scared. I told that it didn't scare me but made me feel good. She said that she was happy that I was comforted by Grandpa.

John F. Kennedy

The next time that I remember experiencing death was the day that John F. Kennedy died. I was at school and very excited because we were having a Girl Scout ceremony after school and all of the parents were coming in to see it. I remember sitting in my fourth-grade class when the teacher was called out to the hall to speak with someone. When she came in we could see that she had been crying. She told us the news.

After school, we held the Girl Scout ceremony. We all gathered in a circle, held hands and sang This Land is Our Land. I swear that everyone in the gymnasium cried. That was the first time I saw death as truly sad.

The next days were filled with news broadcasts of the assassination, Americans from all over the country wept. The impact on me and other children was profound. Somehow, I knew that I would never look at death the same way again. It was much more than going to the ground and then up to God in Heaven.

I think we can all relate to the first death that we experience that impacts a large number of people. We remember the moment we learned of it, where we were at the time, and who we were with. The entire event becomes an experience of growth and maturity. The world is never the same again. Think about what that experience was for you. Was it when John F. Kennedy died? Was it when Elvis died? Maybe it was the Challenger Space Shuttle disaster. Maybe it was on 9-11. Every person in every generation experiences that newsworthy death that changes our lives in a way that prevents us from ever going back. We experience the loss of innocence.

Pal Boy

My little Boston Terrier, Pal Boy, was getting older. I was aware that he had some health problems that my parents were trying to take care of, and they brought him to the veterinarian several times. I was only about nine years old and didn't understand what was wrong with him, but I remember praying that he would be alright.

One day when my brother and I came home from school he was still at the veterinarian's office. My parents waited until after we had eaten dinner. My father went into Eddy's room with him and my mother took me to my room. They simultaneously told us that the doctor had to put Pal to sleep. I remember telling my mother that he should wake him up now. As she tried to explain what had happened, I started crying. I knew what she meant, but I couldn't stand to hear it. I heard my bother begin to yell from his room as my father tried to calm him down.

This was the hardest lesson in death that I had been dealt so far. I was much more aware since John F. Kennedy had died. I understood the permanence of death now. Pal had been my most consistent companion since the day I was born. I didn't think I could handle the loss.

I remember going to school the next day. I kept starting to cry and couldn't concentrate on anything. My teacher brought me to the office. The principle, who was a very kind and soft-spoken man, asked what was wrong. I couldn't answer because I was afraid to cry more. He asked me if everything was okay at home. That's when I told him that my dog had died. He looked at me with total sympathy and understanding. Then he called my mother and asked her to bring me home. I remember him telling her that I was too sad to be in school. This was my first experience of feeling grief and I couldn't understand my emotions.

Eddy wanted my parents to get another dog, but I wasn't ready to love another dog yet. My parents decided that Pal was the last dog they would have. Eddy and I both vowed that when we grew up and had our own homes we would get dogs. I guess that looking forward to a future that included dogs was part of the healing process for us.

Henry

Around 1965 my brother, Eddy, became very good friends with a boy two houses down from us named Henry. Henry had a heart disorder. I never really knew what the problem was, but he had been pretty much confined to his house most of his childhood. Henry underwent a successful open-heart surgery in Boston. He came back home and was told to recover and get strong by exercising and being busy. He got very strong and would go hunting and fishing with Eddy. I remember my parents brought us all deep sea fishing out of Hampton, NH.

Henry was like another brother to me and my whole family loved him dearly. In 1968, at the age of twenty-one, he went back to Boston for the second part of the open-heart surgery. He came through the surgery with flying colors and we were told that he was doing well. A couple of days later we were told that he had developed pneumonia and had died. I felt devastated. This time death hurt. It hurt deeply. I felt like I had lost a brother. In a way, I had.

About a year later I was at a party at a girlfriend's house. Someone pulled out a Ouija board and we all took turns playing with it and giggling. When it was my turn at the board I thought this was silly. I barely touched the planchette when it actually started to move. I asked who was with me and it spelled out H-E-N-R-Y!! The board said that he was with me and watching over me. We all sort of freaked out and I let go of the planchette and wouldn't go back to it. I'm not saying that I believe in Ouija boards, but just that this is my experience with them.

Bobby

I had a friend named Bobby when I was very young, but his family moved to Maryland when his father was transferred for work. One day in high school I heard that there was a new boy in the school. I saw him and thought he looked vaguely familiar. I approached him and asked if we knew each other. He told me his name was Bob and that he lived in town a long time before. When we realized that we were already friends it just became the natural thing to spend a lot of time together.

He wanted me to date him, but I already had a boyfriend so we remained just friends. We became very good friends, and nothing more, but he always let me know that he wanted to be my boyfriend. After a time, I told him that if he was going to keep insisting that I go out with him that I would have no choice but to stop seeing him even as a friend. It was a difficult thing to do, but I stuck to my decision.

A few months later I heard from a mutual friend that Bob had died. He was at a lake up north with his parents when he drowned in the lake. I remember the funeral and that I was so sad. I wanted my friend back. I remember looking at his mother at the wake. I didn't think I had ever seen anyone grieve so deeply. I knew that I was sad, but I couldn't imagine the depth of her sorrow.

My Father

Of eleven children in my father's family that lived to adulthood, my father was one of six that developed Alzheimer's Disease. He was diagnosed in 1995. I helped my mother to deal with the progression of the disease. I started taking her to an Alzheimer's Support Group to help her understand how to deal with the progression of his disease and to better cope with the changes. She started to really enjoy the meetings and looked forward to seeing everyone once a month.

My father had seen several of his siblings with the disease and he used to say, "I pray to God that I don't live long enough to get as bad as they did." He also often told us that when it was his time to go that he wanted us to let him go. He was clear that he did not want to have his life extended with any heroic measures.

By the summer of 1999, my father had started going to an adult day care program. He absolutely loved it there and spoke of the men being the best workers he had ever worked with. Like many people in adult day care he thought he was going to his job when he went there.

On a Thursday in October of 1999, my father had a massive stroke and went into a coma. I will never forget the kind nurse practitioner who told me that he would choose the moment that he would pass. She said that everyone chooses that time for themselves. She said, "He might go when there is a crowd here, when there are only certain people, or when he is alone, but it is in his hands now."

For four days my mother, Eddy, and I took turns holding vigil by his bedside in the hospital. We kept him hydrated, but as he had wanted, we did not extend his life. It was his time, and it was our responsibility to help him pass peacefully. Several family members came to see him, including his grandchildren from Florida.

By Sunday morning his breathing was very shallow and we were told he wouldn't make it through the day. I knew that a lot of people were coming in to see him that day so I brought his shaver in and I shaved him. As I did he lifted his chin so I could shave his neck and moved his head so I could reach places on his face. Even in a coma, he reacted appropriately to the feeling. I was determined to make him presentable. My father never went out in public without being clean and neat, and I would be damned if I was going to let him be seen any other way even if he was on his deathbed.

That afternoon he had a room full of visitors. Everyone was talking and laughing. It had the feeling of a party; a celebration of his life as we told stories about him and spoke to him. I noticed that he had gotten color back in his cheeks and his breathing improved. I asked everyone to take a minute and look at him; at how natural and happy he looked. He was enjoying his company.

The next morning, I stopped in to see him before I went to work. I knew that I had to leave, but I would be back in a couple of hours. I bent to his ear and asked him to hang in there a little while longer and I would get back as soon as I could. I was back in his room by noon. My mother and Eddy were there also. Eddy told me that they had both told him that he could let go now. I held his right hand and my mother held his left hand. Eddy sat at the foot of the bed. Here we were, the immediate family, all together. I leaned over and told him that I loved him and that we were all together now. I told him it was alright to go now. He took a deep breath and then his breaths became further and further apart. It only took a few minutes before he took his last breath. He had chosen his moment, just as the nurse had said that he would.

My father's death was the hardest thing I ever had to deal with. I couldn't comprehend my life without him in it. The pain I felt for weeks and months seemed unbearable at times. At times I felt that I couldn't go on, but I knew that my mother needed me more now than ever. I remember looking at my husband and telling him that for the first time in my life I understood the difference between grieving and mourning. To me, the act of mourning seemed deeper, longer, and more intense than the sadness of grief.

About three months after my father died I was sitting with my mother and we were going over some financial things and trying to get things in order. She told me that she didn't know what she was going to do. I looked at her and promised her that she would never have to worry. I told her that I would help her and take care of her until the day she dies. She said that she wanted to be treated the same way that Dad had been treated. She said that when it is her time that I need to let her die. She told me that she did not want to be kept alive even a minute longer than her time. I told her that I would let her die with as much dignity as my father had. She said that it made her happy to know that I understood her wishes. We talked about dad saying that he prayed to God that he would die before the Alzheimer's progressed. We acknowledged that his prayers had been answered.

Around this time a well-known psychic, John Edward, became popular on television. He would hold group readings where he would stand on a stage in the middle of a room with people seated around the room. He would "feel" a presence in a certain area of the audience and describe the connection he was feeling. Someone in the audience would speak up if they related to it and he would tell them messages from beyond. At the end of the show, the participants would be interviewed so that they could describe the relevance of his reading. I felt mesmerized by this. I wanted to meet him and have a reading with him, but I knew I couldn't afford it. I read his books and felt that somehow, I related to this. I wanted my father to come through in the worst way. I wanted a message from him.

The February after my father died I attended a meeting that was held in a nearby town. A well-known local psychic medium named Gary McKinstry would be there. Gary has some local notoriety with several local radio shows and conducts private and group readings. He is also known for his "Connections" events, in which he connects with several audience members.

I arrived and found a seat. There were probably about fifty people in the room. I was really hoping for a message from my father. I even had a few of my father's belongings with me to try and invite him to me.

Well, I did get a reading that night, but not from my father. My

Memere, his mother, came through. I knew it was her because Gary described her appearance and the way she dressed. He went on to describe in great detail the driveway up to her house, the entrance into her kitchen, the old wringer washing machine she had in the kitchen, and even the things she used to bake for me. Her message for me included that I would soon learn that I am of Native American descent. She also said that I would learn in the coming months that there was a "break" in my family and that there was something I did not know about my name.

A few months later a distant cousin of mine introduced himself to me. This cousin's family was my father's cousins. He told me that he had been working on the genealogy of the family and that we had ancestors who were Native American. I was shocked that the psychic's prediction had come to fruition.

A year after my father died we interred his ashes in the town cemetery. It was a private ceremony with the immediate family and a few of his siblings and a couple of cousins. After we said a few words we were asked to walk away so that they could bury his urn. As we all walked through the cemetery my uncle pointed out a gravestone with a name that I did not recognize. He told me that it was the stone from my great-grandmother. I didn't understand because her name wasn't the same as mine. He explained that she had gotten pregnant and no one knew the name of my Pepere's father. Her maiden name was Brunell, and that is where our family name came from. She didn't marry until my Pepere was around seven years old. I was shocked! Another of Gary's predictions had just come true! I had now learned about the "break in the family name".

When we returned to the burial spot my Uncle leaned toward me and said that he didn't want to offend me, but he and my dad had made a pact a long time ago that whichever one died first the other would dance on his grave to celebrate his life. He asked me to excuse him as he began to do a little jig on my father's grave. We all chuckled because the two of them were always jokesters and always making everyone laugh.

About a year and a half later I still felt my grief very deeply. I was getting ready for work one morning when I looked out my kitchen window. I hadn't thought about the interment of his ashes in a very long time. Suddenly I had an image cross my mind of my Uncle dancing that jig on dad's grave. It was a vision so realistic that I felt transported back to that moment. As I stood there I heard my father's laugh, as clear as day! I whipped around, expecting to see him standing in front of me. Of course, he wasn't there physically, but I swear I felt him in the room. I can honestly say that day was the day I started to feel my grief dissipate, and the healing began.

Eddy

My brother, Eddy, had been sick in the 1980's with cancer. He was in remission, but cancer left him with only fifty percent function of one kidney. By 1999 he was in renal failure and on dialysis three times per week. He started declining more after my father died and eventually moved in with my mother. In her eighties she found herself helping her son and caring for him as he declined.

By 2004 I was in the process of divorcing my first husband after 30 years of marriage. It was a very difficult time and I remember feeling that the separation felt like cutting off my right arm. Once again, I thought I could never feel this much sorrow and pain. I knew the divorce was the right thing to do, but damn, it hurt.

Eddy was getting sicker and my mom was having more difficulty dealing with all of it. That summer Eddy died of complications from renal failure. I delivered his eulogy, reminiscing about growing up; our teen years when my big brother was my best friend and would protect me from the world. I wondered who would protect me now. I felt extremely lonely and vulnerable.

My mother and I struggled to sort out Eddy's belongings. The difficulty included giving most of his things to his ex-girlfriend and her children, whom Eddy considered his children, as he loved them dearly. I really felt like I needed help, but there was no one to help me lifting and sorting his belongings. My sister's first husband, Rosy, called me. I had maintained a good relationship with him even though he and my sister had divorced many years before. He offered to help us. He came to my mother's house when they came to take Eddy's belongings away, and he stayed with us to make sure everything was done properly. I honestly don't know what I would have done without his help.

In the years to follow Rosy was always there whenever my mother or I needed help. He was a great guy. Whenever you would ask Rosy, "How are you?", he would reply, "The best." And he was.

Part II

Rising Tides and Shifting Sands

Changes

Megan's senior class photo, which was also her obituary photo.
She is wearing the sunshine pendant from Provincetown.

I was starting to feel very alone in the world. My mother and my daughters were the most important people in my life. My daughter,

Megan, still lived with me as she was a senior in high school. My daughter, Sarah, was living in Arizona with her husband. My sister was living in Florida, along with two of my nieces and my nephew. My third niece, Darleen, was living in New Hampshire with her husband.

Megan and I became closer than ever during the two years that I was going through my divorce. We bonded in so many ways while we were living alone together in our home. One day she said that there was a song she wanted to play for me because it felt like "us" and it related to everything that was going on around us. She was on YouTube at the time. She played the song by Rodney Atkins *If You're Going Through Hell*. I had to laugh because country music was not her usual choice in music and because the song really did fit our life right then.

I took Megan on a mother-daughter getaway to Cape Cod in August of 2004. We went to the beach and shopped. We just enjoyed girl time together. One day I drove us to Provincetown to explore. We went through the shops and Megan found a sterling silver pendant of the sun that she loved so I bought it for her.

I had been making jewelry for about ten years by then as a hobby and for gifts and I was intent on finding some unique beads in Provincetown. I was surprised that there weren't any real bead stores there. Eventually, I found some sea glass beads. I bought a handful of them in a deep blue and some in an off-white color. Megan asked what I was going to make with them because there weren't enough to make a necklace. I told her that I would save them until the right project came along and then they would be perfect. She laughed at me because she knew how obsessed I could be of beads and jewelry making. Later that day we climbed up the Provincetown monument to look out at the ocean. A picture I asked a stranger to take of us is still one of my favorite pictures of the two of us together. It was the perfect ending to a perfect summer day.

By 2005 the divorce was final. The day of the divorce I went home and literally crawled into bed and pulled the covers up. I fell asleep for about an hour. When I woke Megan was standing at the foot of my bed and asked how it went. I told her it was over. She climbed into bed with me and put her arms around me. I told her that we would be able to stay in the house for at least one more year and that her dad and I would be splitting her college expenses. These were the two most important things in the world to her at that time. I looked at her and saw tears streaming down her cheeks. She looked up at me and said, "Mom, you are the strongest woman in the world to me and I love you so much." That was all I needed to go on.

A couple of months later I met Steve. Our romance was like a whirlwind in my life. We both fell madly in love almost immediately after we met. I couldn't remember ever feeling this happy. Steve formed a wonderful relationship with my mother and daughters. He and Megan had some really deep conversations and he became a strong male influence in her life.

In October of 2006, Steve and I went on a Caribbean cruise together. One evening after dinner we walked out to the stern of the ship. There was no one else around, the deck was empty. The bartender was cleaning up. A Frank Sinatra song was playing in the background. We looked out and saw the moon reflecting off the water. Steve turned to me and in that moment, he asked me to marry him. It was the most romantic moment in my life. I felt completely swept off my feet and deeply in love. Life couldn't get any better than this, could it? The next day we docked in Grand Cayman and picked out a diamond ring.

In the beginning of 2007, Sarah called from her home in Texas. She spoke with Megan first. Megan kept looking at me with a really weird look on her face. I really wondered what they were cooking up. Then Megan handed me the phone and I had my turn to talk with Sarah. That's when Sarah announced that she was pregnant. Life just kept getting better and better.

Megan started planning a shower for Sarah. She had loads of ideas for it and started buying toys and things for her new baby nephew. Yes! It's a boy! Since Sarah's husband was being deployed to Iraq, she and Megan made plans for Megan to fly to Texas in May when her semester ended and help Sarah move back home to have her baby here with family around. She had even bought an airplane ticket.

Megan was very excited about her upcoming trip to Texas and had made a mix music CD of country songs. She had told Sarah that she was going to play the CD while in Texas. Country music again! By this time Megan was definitely beginning to expand her taste in music. She especially liked the song *Save a Horse, Ride a Cowboy* by Big and Rich. I always thought this song was a little off, but pretty funny. Megan seemed to also see the humor in it.

Megan

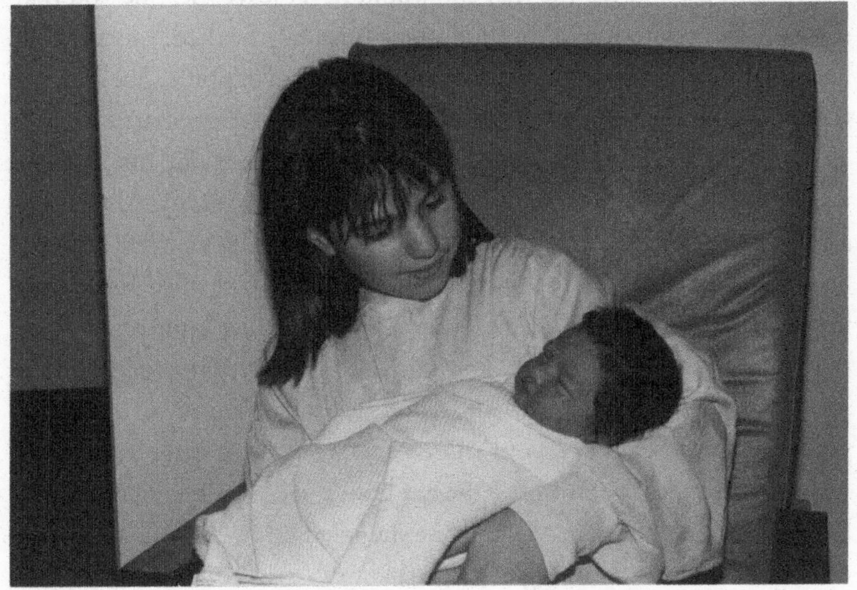

Sarah holding Megan at one hour old.

Megan was a February baby. I used to joke that Sarah was born in a heat wave and Megan was born in a blizzard. I joked about it, but it was the truth. In many ways, they were complete opposites, but in other ways, they were like two versions of the same girl. They were almost ten years apart so the differences were very apparent, but the core of their personalities was very similar. I remember days when the biggest argument in our home was whether we would watch Sesame Street or MTV. Those were the days. Why can't life always be that simple? Megan had a Big Bird stuffed toy that she carried with her everywhere she went. I had difficulty even getting it away from her to clean it. I guess it was her version of a security blanket.

When Megan was little she would dress up in frilly little dresses and dance around all day. She would ask us to videotape her and tell us to write on the tape that it was "Megan's magical dance". Later she added fairy wings, she had several sets of various colors to match her dresses. A magic wand and magic fairy dust were also added to her dance. She told me that someday she wanted to be a fairy and dance all day and perform magic. Her imagination was boundless.

Megan used to tell me that she would never leave me. She said that she would live with me in this house until the day she died. I used to tell her that when she got older she would want her own home. She insisted that would never happen. She was going to stay here no matter what.

She started asking for a puppy at around five years old. She said she wanted the kind of dog that would always be like a puppy. About that same time a nurse I worked with told me that she had a litter of pups. She bred Beagles, but somehow it seemed that her Yorkshire Terrier had impregnated one of the beagles and the result was a litter of adorable puppies that she couldn't sell as purebreds. Sarah, Megan, and I went to see the puppies and picked a male out of the litter of four. By the time we got home we had changed our minds and wanted the only female, the runt of the litter. When I brought her home, she bonded with all of us but was inseparable from Megan. She snuggled up to her constantly. We decided to name her Snuggles since that's what she did best. Snuggles was the best little dog. When she ran it looked more like a bunny that was hopping than a dog.

As Megan got a little older she made a lot of friends in school and in the Girl Scouts. Even at a very young age she placed a high value on her friendships and would be true to her friends even if they had argued. She would be so sad whenever she felt that a friend had been unfair to her, but then she would forgive them just as easily.

Megan with her friend, Jeanine at their Junior Prom

In high school, she got a job working at a local child care center. She loved working there and the children loved her. For her prom in October of her junior year of high school, she had gotten a beautiful gown. It was satin and bright turquoise. She got high heels that were covered in rhinestones. With her blonde hair, she looked like Cinderella in it. Since there was a Halloween party at the daycare center the following week she thought it would be fun to wear her gown one more time. When she arrived at work for the party the children were so excited because they said she was the best Cinderella ever! She loved making them happy.

Two sisters at the day care center became especially close to her. She started to babysit for them on some weekends. The older one seemed to really look up to her and she became almost a mentor to her or a big sister.

When it was time for Megan to get her driving license I was as nervous as any parent. I took her for rides on the back roads of our town so she could get used to the feeling of driving and she really did well. She got her license and was on her way.

After she graduated from high school she had to leave the job at the daycare because she went away to Framingham State College for her freshman year. She enjoyed her classes at Framingham but was very homesick. The summer after her freshman year she asked me if I would be disappointed in her if she didn't go back there. I suggested that she might want to look into a school closer to home. She ended up transferring to Eastern Connecticut State University in time to start her Sophomore year. She was really happy that she would be able to stay at home and commute to school. Of course, now she really needed a car she could call her own because she would be commuting daily. That's when I bought a new car and gave her mine to drive. I kept it in my name, but it was hers for all intents and purposes.

Once she moved back home and started commuting to Eastern she was able to start babysitting once again for the two sisters who had become so close to her. She would go to their house to get them off of the school bus and stay with them until their parents got home from work.

February 9, 2007, Megan turned twenty years old. She wanted to go to her favorite Japanese restaurant in Worcester to celebrate. She invited two of her closest friends, Denise and Jeanine to come with us. My mother came, and of course, Steve and I were there. It was a small group, but we had a really good time.

Also in February of 2007, she came home one day to tell me about a friend of hers who had died in a car accident. Megan was very upset and decided to go to the funeral. I couldn't go because I had plans for that evening. I have regretted ever since then that I didn't go. If I knew then what I know now, I definitely would have gone to the funeral. Megan came home after the funeral and sat on the loveseat while I was sitting on the couch. She began telling me about it, about how painful it was for her to deal with the death of a friend. I talked to her about Henry and Bobby and how I felt losing friends when I was young. She told me the songs they played at the funeral and about her friend's parents. She started to cry; cries that turned to hysterics. I moved over to the love seat and took her in my arms and held her tight. It was heartbreaking to hear of the pain the parents were experiencing and to see the pain Megan felt. I couldn't imagine losing her; I started to cry with her and we held tightly to each other. She looked up at me and said, "I promise you that I will always drive carefully because I never want to think that I died in an accident and made you as sad as her parents. I'll never let that happen."

Around then I started to clean out the closet in the spare bedroom to prepare for Sarah to come home. It was full of clothes and toys from both girls' childhood. I came across Megan's stuffed Big Bird toy and called her in. "Hey, remember this guy? Do you want me to donate him?" She took Big Bird and hugged him close and said, "No way! I'm keeping my Big Bird until I die!" Then she laughed and took him into her bedroom for safe keeping.

To understand the impact that Megan's life had you would need to know some of the things that mattered to her. When she transferred in her Sophomore year to Eastern she started volunteering as the Planned Parenthood Student Intern. She would set up tables around the campus representing Planned Parenthood and hand out condoms and speak about birth control, STDs, and other pertinent subjects. Her goal was to promote safe sex and distribute knowledge about reproductive health. She took this responsibility very seriously and was very proud of it. She set up an email address to provide answers to student's concerns that would be kept completely confidential. She also spent a little time volunteering at a Planned Parenthood clinic, an HIV/AIDs clinic and volunteered in the Women's Center at Eastern.

Megan with Betty DeGeneres at Eastern CT State University.

One of the highlights of her year at Eastern came when Betty DeGeneres, Ellen DeGeneres' mother, was scheduled to speak on campus. Ms. Degeneres wrote a book about Ellen, titled *"Love, Ellen"*. Ellen was always one of Megan's heroines. Megan had worked so hard for LGBT rights and idolized Ellen as a strong female influence. Megan was honored when she was asked by the Women's Center to be Ms. DeGeneres' guide before and after her talk. Megan also assisted during the book signing. She felt like a celebrity and couldn't believe she was spending time with the mother of one of her idols.

In her Spring semester, she was accepted into the Social Work degree program. She had very clear goals for herself. She planned to get her Master's Degree and be a social worker at Planned Parenthood when she graduated. I have no doubt she would have reached this goal and she probably would have worked for Planned Parenthood after graduation.

There was a construction company clearing the woods across the road from our house and putting in house lots for a new development. There were signs up designating the lots available for sale. One day in early April, as the final trace of snow was melting and the New England Spring made the ground thick with mud, Megan decided it would be fun to drive up into the woods and check out the house lots. She got her car stuck in the mud up to the tire rims and couldn't get it out. Apparently, she had to call AAA and get it towed. I spoke with Megan and told her how angry I felt about her doing that. I felt like I should punish her, but I really had not had to punish her much, and I couldn't remember the last time I had felt the need to do so. Once again, she sat on the love seat and I sat on the couch and we talked. She cried and said how terrible she felt about doing such a stupid thing. She said that she knew she was a smart girl, but sometimes she just did stupid things and she was very sorry. She said, "I worry that someday I will die and people will only remember the stupid stuff I've done and not any of the good stuff." I felt so bad for her because she was truly remorseful for her actions. She had put so much work into good deeds, but she really was just a young girl still. Young girls, all young people, do stupid stuff. Megan was just a regular kid, doing regular stuff. Once again, I sat next to her on the loveseat and assured her that she would never be remembered just for doing stupid stuff. I didn't have any idea then that she had less than two weeks left on Earth.

On April twentieth I learned of an auto accident near my place of work where several teenagers died as a result. I was very upset and spoke with Megan about it. These were really good kids. They had not been drinking or doing anything wrong. The way I understood it, they had gone out for ice cream and realized that they were going to be late getting home so they were speeding, trying to get home quickly. I remember thinking that I felt terrible for their parents, but of course, I was glad it wasn't me. My child was safe.

Twenty-Four Hours

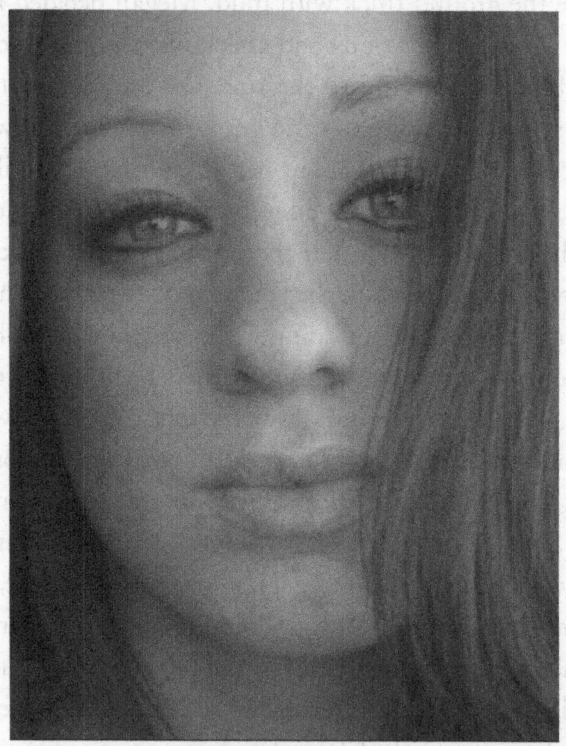

A "selfie" Megan took while sitting in the car two weeks prior to her accident.

On April 26, 2007, Steve and I had just booked a venue for our wedding, which we had decided would take place on April 27, 2008. We sat down with a glass of wine and toasted the life we were planning and talked about how happy we were–how wonderful everything was.

Megan came home that night as we were getting ready for bed. She was sitting on the top step as I walked out of the second-floor bathroom.

She told me that she had a cold and was really tired. She laid down on the rug and waved her hand into my bedroom and said, "Goodnight, Steve". We all retired.

In the morning Steve left for work, as usual. I was getting ready for work when Megan came down to have breakfast. I asked her what she was doing that day. She planned to take my mother to a doctor appointment, go to school, and babysit in the afternoon. She said that she would be home by 6:30 in the evening.

As I stood in the doorway leaving for work I looked at her standing there in the kitchen. I will never forget how she looked. Her hair was up in a loose bun with strands falling around her face. She wore a pink and white striped souvenir t-shirt I had bought her on our cruise and pink sweatpants that she had slept in. I told her to drive carefully, it was raining and the roads could be slippery. She looked at me and said, "Oh, Mom, nothing's going to happen to me." I asked her to humor me and drive slow and carefully. She said, "I'll see you tonight. Don't worry, I love you, Mommy." I said, "I love you, too."

I worked all day and was surprised at how well the day went. It was a Friday, which was usually the toughest day of the week for me as an Admissions Coordinator for a long-term acute care hospital. I actually left work on time, which was unusual. Steve and I met at the local gym that we belonged to. One of the first things he said to me was that our neighbor had come over and said that the state police were at the house earlier and they were trying to find my ex-husband, Megan and Sarah's father. We commented on the fact that we couldn't imagine why they would be looking for him. We had certainly had our differences, but he had never been in trouble with the law.

As I walked back to my car my cell phone rang; it was Sarah. She told me that her father had called and wanted my cell phone number because he had to reach me. I told her about the police looking for him and said that I would figure something out when I got home and would talk to her later.

When I got home at 6:15 Steve suggested that I call the state police barracks and showed me the business card the officer had left for me. I thought I should call my ex-husband first and find out why they were looking for him. Just then I saw his car pull into the driveway. Now I really knew something was wrong. After one of our last arguments, he had said that he would never again come to the house.

He knocked on the door and I let him in. He told me to sit down. I looked at him and said, "You look like the one who needs to sit down. You look like Hell. Do you know the state police are looking for you?" We sat next to each other at the dining room table while Steve watched from the kitchen. He told me that there had been an accident. I asked if someone in his family was hurt. He said that Megan was in the car. I told him that was impossible, that she took my mother to the doctor and then went to school. I told him that she was babysitting and would be home at 6:30. He said, "Megan is not coming home." I told him that he was wrong and he would see because she would be there in just a few minutes. He looked at me and said, "Sue, Megan is never coming home again. She died today." I screamed at him, I cried, I said that he was wrong and that it was impossible. He held me as we both fell apart and I looked past him to see Steve standing there shaking his head with tears streaming down his cheeks.

In that moment time stopped and yet it was rushing past me. Every single bit of my being was out of control. To this day I cannot recall it without shaking.

Then I became aware of a knocking on the door. I turned around and saw a state police officer at my door. I answered the door and he entered. He told us about the accident. It was raining when she had been driving to school. There was an area of the road that had recently been repaired which flooded when it rained. It was on Route 198 in Chaplin, CT. There is a bridge there that crosses over a part of the river where the water under it swirls. They call it Diana's Pool. When she got to that area she hydroplaned and spun around. The passenger side of her car was hit by a Ford F350 truck that was traveling in the opposite direction. I was told that she had died immediately. The first 911 call had come in at 10:27 A.M.

We asked if we could go somewhere and see her. She had been taken directly to the state coroner's office and there was no way we could see her. The coroner's office was closed by the time we knew of her death.

We were also told that if we went the next morning that we would only see her through a monitor in the morgue. She was already scheduled for an autopsy the next morning which was required by law since she died outside of a hospital.

I wondered how she could have been dead for eight hours before I knew about it. I understand the logistics of it. The police found her identification and came to the house, but no one was home. They didn't know how to reach me and none of the neighbors had my work telephone number. They attempted to contact her father at his place of work, but the policy there was to inform him when he left at 3:30 that he had a message to contact the police. He had finally made contact with the police around 4:00. He had been trying to find me since then. He wanted me to hear it from him instead of from the police or a stranger. Regardless of any of the problems we went through I respect him for doing that.

But still, how did I not know for eight hours that my daughter had died? Megan and I were very close. I think we had talked about everything in our lives. We had a deep love and connection. I felt like I should have known, I should have sensed that something was wrong. I've always had a sense of things. An ESP, or something. Why didn't I on that day? I'll never know.

Together her father and I called Sarah and had to tell her over the phone that her sister had died. It was the hardest and worst telephone call in my life. Then we drove to my mother's house to tell her. I wondered how I could tell my eighty-six-year-old mother that her granddaughter had died. My mother was always the strongest woman I have ever known. She cried, but she handled it well. I asked her if she wanted to come to my home for the night. I was afraid to leave her alone, but she insisted on staying in her own home.

When I got home I found out that my neighbors had called to ask if we found out why the police had been around. Steve told them about Megan. We had been neighbors since Megan and their daughters were little. The girls had all grown up together. The next thing I knew they all came over. Honestly, I didn't feel like I could face anyone that night, but I found comfort in their presence as we all cried together.

When everyone had left and it was time to get ready for bed I went upstairs for the first time since getting home. I have a dressing table in my bedroom, but I didn't have a seat for it at the time so I had been using a small wicker bench which fits right under it nicely. Sitting at the table was where I always put on my make up in the morning.

Megan had gotten in the habit of doing her makeup there, also. She had a bad habit of leaving the bench sticking straight out the long way. I had told her time and again that I didn't mind her using my mirror, but please put the bench back the way it belongs so I wouldn't trip over it. I walked into my room and there was the bench sticking straight out. That's when I really fell apart for the first time. I realized that was one of the last places she had sat at home. She had touched all of the things on the table just hours before. The hardest part was realizing she would never sit there and leave that bench sticking out again. How did I go from ecstatically planning my wedding and the birth of my first grandchild to complete devastation in twenty-four hours?

Going Through the Motions

The next day Megan's father and I met with the funeral director and made the arrangements. I didn't know whether I should have Megan buried or cremated. My father and brother were cremated, and I knew my mother had chosen to be cremated when she died. We made partial arrangements and left to think about the rest of the arrangements.

The next few days passed in a blur of condolences, calls, and drop in visitors as the news of Megan's death circulated. Sarah flew home from Texas. Everything seemed surreal. How could this be happening? I felt like I was living some alternate life and my beautiful little girl would come walking through the door at any minute and tell me it was all a mistake. They had the wrong girl. I knew that had to be the real truth. This wasn't possible.

One visitor who dropped in with a beautiful bouquet of pink roses was a lady that I didn't even recognize at first. She introduced herself as one of Megan's past teachers. She had taken Megan shopping on a few occasions and they had kept in touch for several years. In fact, Megan had emailed her a few times a week for years. They loved and respected each other. She asked me about the funeral plans and I told her that I didn't know if I should cremate Megan or not. She apologized and said that she hoped I would not be offended by what she was about to tell me. She didn't want to hurt my feelings. She told me that Megan wanted to be cremated. They had had that discussion. I couldn't believe what I was hearing. How could I be hurt or offended? Knowing what Megan wanted was such valuable information. Now I knew what I needed to do.

They always say that you should talk about your wishes with people who will make decisions and plans for you someday. Who would ever think at twenty years old that you would have the need to discuss this with someone? I'm sure that Megan didn't think she needed to tell anyone, but I am so grateful that she did.

On Sunday we invited Megan's friends to the house. After all, they were grieving also. We all sat in the dining room and talked about Megan. We laughed and cried together. We all bonded over our love of Megan and the deep loss we were all experiencing. I think it was one of the times when I felt the most comforted through those first few days. One of her friends said that they wanted to ask me a question. They wanted to know if I would be offended if they wore pink to her funeral. It was her favorite color and they wanted to honor her in this way. I told them that I thought it was the best thing I had heard in days. We decided that we would all wear something pink to her wake and her funeral. By the next day, we had decided to take wearing pink to another level and went to the local craft store and bought all of the pink ribbons they had. We cut foot long pink ribbons to hand out to everyone at the wake. I didn't honestly know how many we would need, but we prepared hundreds of them.

On Monday we had to go to the Connecticut State Police barracks. They needed us to give a report of everything we knew about her last twenty-four hours. I told them about coming home around nine o'clock the night before; she had gone to dinner with a friend. I was asked to inform her friend that she might need to go to the police barracks to give a statement, also. That was never necessary because the blood results did not show any drugs or alcohol in her blood except for caffeine and a cold medication I had given her that morning. I told them about the last morning and the things we had said to each other. I told them that her last words to me were "I love you."

Her father told them that he had spoken to her on her cell phone just minutes before the accident. Yes, she must have been on her phone while she was driving, but they had hung up about ten minutes before the accident. The police officer wrote everything down and asked us to sign the statement. Then he handed me a bag of items they had taken out of her car. It held her purse, wallet, laptop, some CDs, shoes, school books, and notebooks. They were all in individual plastic bags and labeled "evidence". I told him that this couldn't be happening. He said that he was sorry. He said that this is the worst part of his job, and he wished he never had to do this. We asked to see the car and he said that it was in the parking lot behind the police barracks, but he advised us not to look at it because it might be too upsetting.

After we signed the statement, the officer told me that he had to say something to me that might be very upsetting, but he felt he needed to mention it. I told him that there was nothing he could say to me about Megan that would surprise me; I knew her very well and he could say anything. He was very careful choosing his words as he told me that they had found certain items in her car that probably didn't belong there and they weren't sure what to think of it. I told him to just say it; what was in her car? He said that in the back (it was a station wagon) they had found cases of condoms! They couldn't figure out why a twenty-year-old would need cases of condoms. As serious as this situation was when I look back at this moment I have to chuckle to myself. It was almost like Megan left a joke in her wake. I explained her role in Planned Parenthood to him and told him that I would need to take the condoms back as they were the property of Planned Parenthood and I would need to return them.

The funeral director prepared her so that we could have a private viewing. He explained that her injuries would prevent her from having an open coffin for the public. The reason was that after preparing her we would not be able to touch her at all. He was explicit in his directions. Apparently, touching her might reveal something that would be very disturbing for us to witness, but he had managed to prepare her in a way that we could at least see her.

I had to pick out clothes for her to be laid out in. How do I do this? There was a cream-colored lace dress that still had the tags on it. No, I couldn't picture her in that. She had just bought a pair of dressy grey pants. She had said, "Well, if I'm going to be a social worker, I guess I should start dressing like one!" I guess those would be good to bring. She had a beautiful pink satin blouse–that works. What about shoes? I know! The pink high heels–yes! Megan was known for her love of high heels and she was going to wear them now. What about jewelry?

I found the strand of pink pearls I had made for her. She said that she loved wearing them because she felt like she was close to me when she had them on. I would put my arms around her neck with the pink pearls. She would look classy and dignified. I felt like I was missing something, and then I thought of it. I went to her room to find the perfect last accessory. Big Bird was going in her coffin to comfort her on her journey.

We waited all day to be able to see her. It took that long for our funeral director to get her perfect. Steve and I, Sarah, her father, and my mother were all in attendance. No one else saw her in the coffin. The funeral director stood at a distance watching us. At one point I almost touched her arm, but he cleared his voice and when I looked over he just shook his head. I wanted to touch her so desperately, but I couldn't. Hell, I wanted to scoop her up in my arms and hold her once again, but I couldn't. I would hold the memory of, and be comforted by, all the times we had held each other.

The Wake

We had hundreds of pink ribbons to start, but we were not prepared for the number of people that came to the wake. There was a constant line of people through the funeral home and down the street that lasted for about four hours. Literally, hundreds of people attended. The funeral director estimated well over five hundred people were in attendance.

There were friends of Megan's, family, teachers of hers from kindergarten through college. They came from Framingham State College in Massachusetts and Eastern Connecticut State University, her grammar school, middle school and high school. Even people from the summer camp she used to attend came to her wake. People I had worked with, that her father worked with, and that Steve worked with all came. A dear friend of mine from Florida flew up to be with us. I couldn't even comprehend the number of people whose lives had been touched by Megan.

I had a headache. It was not just any headache, my head felt like it would explode. I couldn't do this! I tried to compose myself, but I was falling apart from the inside out. It felt like there was a volcano inside of me that was ready to erupt. The pressure was intense and it was trying to blow my head off. The sights, the sounds, the flowers, the tears, and all of these people gathering in one place to say goodbye.

At one point a young lady was speaking with Megan's father and I could see that he was having a strong reaction to what she was saying. I walked over to find out who she was as I didn't recognize her from Megan's friends. She told us her name, and she said that she was with Megan when she passed. I was shocked and asked her to explain. She told me that she was driving her car and came up the road right after the impact. She had called 911. She told us that she went to the car and saw Megan. She had told Megan that she was not alone and would stay right there with her. She told us that she watched her take her last breath and kept talking with her until she was sure that she had passed. I cried, both from sadness and from joy. Yes, joy, as difficult as that is to understand. Joy because now I knew that she wasn't alone when she died. I had been so upset that she had died alone with no one to comfort her. I will always feel that Zoe is one of those angels on Earth that we hear about. She is the type of person who stops her own life and provides something to someone else, maybe a complete stranger, without regard to her own needs. She entered Megan's life but for a moment in time, a moment when there was not another single person there for her. And for this, I will always be grateful.

Several years later a co-worker told me that he had been a first responder at an accident in Boston. He had stayed with a young lady until she died in the car. He came to me and asked if he should talk to her parents. He knew that she had not suffered at the end, but thought it might be too difficult for her parents if he talked to them about it. I encouraged him to speak with them. I relayed my story about Zoe and explained that it eased a part of my mind and that I treasure the knowledge I now have of Megan's last moments.

At her wake, there were several people who had traveled from the Southern New England Planned Parenthood Headquarters in New Haven, CT. Megan had been advocating for the passage of a bill that would allow emergency contraception for rape victims. She had written a letter appealing to its passage. At her wake, as the representatives for Planned Parenthood stood in the long line that stretched up the road to enter the funeral home they received a message that the bill had passed! When they spoke to me they told me that Megan was instrumental in passing the bill. Can you even imagine the pride I feel for the good works she accomplished? In just twenty short years she managed to make an impact.

The Funeral

The hardest day of my life arrived. This day I would say goodbye to my baby girl. I wondered how I would even put one foot in front of the other. Our family members met at our house to go to the funeral home together. People gathered at the funeral home and the procession was called. Once everyone else was in their cars we were allowed to say our good-byes to Megan.

She had so many friends and family that it was difficult to decide who should be pallbearers. We decided on over a dozen of her friends and cousins. All of the girls accompanied the coffin into the church with the boys in front of them. Sarah gave a beautiful eulogy and tribute to Megan. I remember her speaking about the process of transitioning from the present to the past tense in regards to Megan's life. She was eloquent in her delivery of her thoughts. When we left the church, the male pallbearers accompanied the coffin and the females followed. I remember walking out with my mother between my niece, Darleen, and me. I was trying to hold up my mother because it felt like she would fall down. I was crying so hard, but I wondered who was going to hold me up.

I stood on the top steps of the church looking down toward the street where the hearse was parked. All of the pallbearers were there, all of them and all of us wearing something pink. The funeral director handed each one of them a pink rose and they took turns placing the roses on her coffin before he closed the doors. I have an image in my mind that plays it over at times. A memory I will never let go of. The pink, grey, black, and white of Megan's funeral. The beauty of it. The tragedy of it.

Part III

Life After Death

Believe

When Megan was a little girl she had a habit of always wanting to succeed at whatever she was currently doing. She ended many sentences with the term, "No matter what!" She didn't do it in a bratty spoiled way, but with determination. She was the type of little girl, then a teenager, and finally young lady with determination. As such, she was successful in many ways. She also told others to think successfully. Her friends called her the cheerleader of their group. She would encourage others to succeed, to strive for more, and to be all they could be.

Megan came home one day with a white painted wooden cutout sign that was about four feet long and about six inches high. It said one word. BELIEVE. I asked what she planned to do with it. She replied that she was going to keep it in her room to remind her that if she believes something is true, she can achieve it. She put it on the windowsill in her bedroom where she would see it every day.

After she died I was in her room. I just sat on her bed, the bed she spent her last night on Earth in. I cried. After a while I noticed something sticking up behind her desk, which was in front of the window. I reached down to see what it was and pulled up the BELIEVE sign. I brought the sign with me to the funeral home and it sat on a shelf above her coffin. When I brought it home I put it on a shelf in my living room to remind me that if I believe something is true, it is true.

Proceeds from the sale of these pink bracelets in Megan's memory contributed to the memorial scholarship fund.

About a week after the funeral I was visited by someone from the high school she had attended. They wanted to run a fundraiser to collect money for a donation to the scholarship fund Sarah and I were forming. They had decided to sell pink bracelets with Megan's initials, MLK, on one side and a short phrase on the other side. They were looking for input on what it should say. We immediately knew it had to say BELIEVE. We were trying to figure out the rest of the phrase when we remembered that we used to call her the "no matter what" kid. Of course, she had grown to be the girl who always encouraged others. The phrase that we chose was "Believe in yourself no matter what". The bracelet sale became a substantial contribution to the Megan L. Kleczka Memorial Scholarship at Eastern Connecticut State University.

Megan taught me and a lot of other people that they can achieve goals if they only believe in themselves and the goals they want to achieve. I also learned that sometimes there are things in life that we can't see, but our belief in them is what makes them real and allows us to see them.

Mother's Day

Mother's Day 2005.

After the funeral, we had the dilemma of helping Sarah move all of her belongings from Texas and back to New England. There would no longer be the opportunity for Megan to fly there and help pack things for the move. There would no longer be a sister road trip playing her country music CD.

It was decided that Sarah and her father would fly to Texas, pack up her belongings and rent a car to move her back to New England. She would live with me until her baby was born and for as long as she wished afterward. They left for their trip within two weeks of the funeral.

They were still in Texas when Mother's Day arrived. I sat on the loveseat in my living room for a very long time. I needed to go see my mother, but I couldn't move. I felt frozen inside. I remembered Mother's Days when I would be instructed to stay in bed listening to the sounds of my family making me breakfast in bed and bringing the Sunday paper to me. It was bittersweet. I felt so incredibly grateful that I had those memories, but I also felt incredibly sad that I would never have those days again.

I was taken out of my reverie by the sound of the telephone ringing. I had no idea who could have been calling me. It was the mother of Megan's friend, who had died in February. She told me that she was sorry for my loss and I told her that I was sorry for hers. I was so thankful that she had reached out to me. We talked for a while about this being the first Mother's Day since our daughters had died. I felt more comfort than I imagined I could. She told me about a parent's grief support group she and her husband had attended in a nearby town and asked if I would like to go. The name of the group is The Compassionate Friends, and it is an international support group for bereaved parents. I had never heard of it, but I was willing to try.

Steve took Sarah and me to the next Compassionate Friends meeting in June. I was surprised to see how many parents were there. I guess I wasn't the only one after all! We all took turns telling the story of our children. One mother was still going to the meetings and it had been twenty years since her child had died. I still couldn't believe that there could possibly be a time when I would be living twenty years without Megan in my life. It was unimaginable.

I never went back to the Compassionate Friends. They are a wonderful support group. A branch of the group is located in most areas. I think it was just too soon for me to attend. It upset me hearing all of the stories of how children had died. I couldn't bear it at that time.

I stayed out of work for almost a month. I just couldn't bring myself to return. I couldn't think, sleep, or eat. I felt immobile. I remember Steve talking to me one day. He made me promise him something. I had to promise that if I ever became sad enough to "do something about it" that I had to tell him so that he could help me. He could see how depressed I felt and he wanted to protect me.

I remember one day I woke and sat on the couch. I sat there, in that same spot the entire day. I was more alone than I had ever felt in my entire life. My mother called about four o'clock in the afternoon and asked what I was doing. Nothing. She asked what I was wearing. Pajamas. She asked what I had eaten. Nothing. She asked what was on TV. Nothing. She asked how I felt. Empty.

Now, my mother was always a stay-at-home mom. She never thought I should work after I had children. To my parents, women stayed home and took care of their families. My mother said something to me that I never thought I would hear her say. She said, "Susan, I want you to call your boss and tell him you are ready to go back to work. Get in there as soon as possible. Pull yourself together before it's too late." This was probably the best piece of advice my mother had ever given to me.

Ready or not, I went back to work. It was very hard to function, but each day that I worked I found myself getting back into the routine and back into life. The struggle to try to function again after a loss this deep feels impossible at the time. However, I believe that getting back to work helped me beyond words. It made it necessary to put one foot in front of the other. It made me think again. I had to process facts and deal with issues throughout the workday. My brain was forced to react to the needs of the job. I couldn't sit and obsess over my loss.

Don't get me wrong, I cried on the way to work and on the way home every day. I cried on my days off. I grieved deep and heavily still. I never denied my grief and sorrow. I just learned to channel the times that I let it take over to appropriate times and circumstances. That's not to say that I didn't have my moments at work, also. I was just fortunate that my co-workers understood and cut me a little slack.

It's a process to learn how to put one step in front of the other; to get through one more minute, hour, one more day. But we learn how to do this. The alternative is to fall prey to depression, and that isn't beneficial to anyone. So, we learn to go on.

Snuggles

In 2007, Snuggles was thirteen years old and definitely acting like an elderly dog. She was having problems with her hip, and we would have to carry her down the five or six steps from the back deck to the yard. Then we would carry her back up the steps. She no longer ran around the yard, bouncing like a bunny rabbit.

Snuggles seemed to know immediately when Megan died. She began walking around the house with her head down. Her eyes watered, as though she was crying. Sometimes she would stare off like she was focusing on something very important, and nothing could take her attention from what she was "seeing". I used to swear she was seeing Megan.

I decided that I wanted to buy a weeping cherry tree with pink blossoms that would bloom in the spring. I wanted to create a memorial garden around the tree. This began a discussion regarding where in the yard the tree and garden should be. I wanted it in a certain corner near the wooded area. My fiancé, Steve, felt it should go in the front yard, and Megan's father thought it should go closer to the road so it could be seen better.

One day when Snuggles asked to go out I opened the door expecting to carry her down the steps, but she surprised me by running down the steps on her own. I followed her. She nearly ran to the wooded area where I thought the memorial garden should go. She stood there, staring at that spot, and refused to move. I tried to call to her to get back in the house, offered her treats, and various other distractions, but she wouldn't move. Finally, I said, "Snuggles, is this where Megan wants the garden?" She immediately turned toward me, looked right at me, she looked back at the spot, then walked back to the house. When Steve got back home I told him that Megan had sent a message through Snuggles, that she wants the garden by the wooded area. He began digging in that area that weekend.

The Coffee House Meeting

There was a coffee shop in the next town from us where Megan loved to meet her friends. They would sit and talk for hours there. Shortly after she died some of her friends asked me to meet them there to visit. We sat and visited for a while and then decided to walk around the town.

We came to a shop in town that a local psychic ran. They wanted to go in. I stood in the doorway. The psychic was talking with the girls and then looked at me. She said, "You have children around you. Are there children you have lost?" I was really taken back by her comments. I said that I had not lost "children". She insisted that I had lost two children, a boy, and a girl. She said that the boy had not been born yet, but that he is still around me.

The odd thing about this is that in 1981 I had a health problem and the doctor said that I might have had a miscarriage, but there was no way of knowing for sure. We hadn't planned to have another baby then, so I never worried about it. No one else knew about this except my first husband.

Also, a friend had brought me to a psychic around the year 2000 who had told me that I had three children. I had insisted that I did not have three children. He told me that I had a dark-haired girl, a light-haired girl, and a boy in between.

Now I stood in this store with another psychic telling me that I had lost a boy! I was shocked.

Megan's friend, Jeanine, decided to make an appointment with the psychic. She reported back to me that a pink cloud was present during the reading, indicating a female presence was with her, but otherwise there was nothing relevant to Megan having come through.

It wasn't until several years later when I asked her if there had been anything else at all that was said during that reading. Jeanine said nothing except some ridiculous thing about her being with some big yellow bird. I was shocked and said, "Oh my God, that's Big Bird!" Jeanine insisted, "No, not Big Bird, just some yellow bird." She was shocked when I told her that Big Bird was in her coffin with her, and I told her the story behind that. Remember, it was a closed coffin so no one knew about that except for the few of us who viewed her.

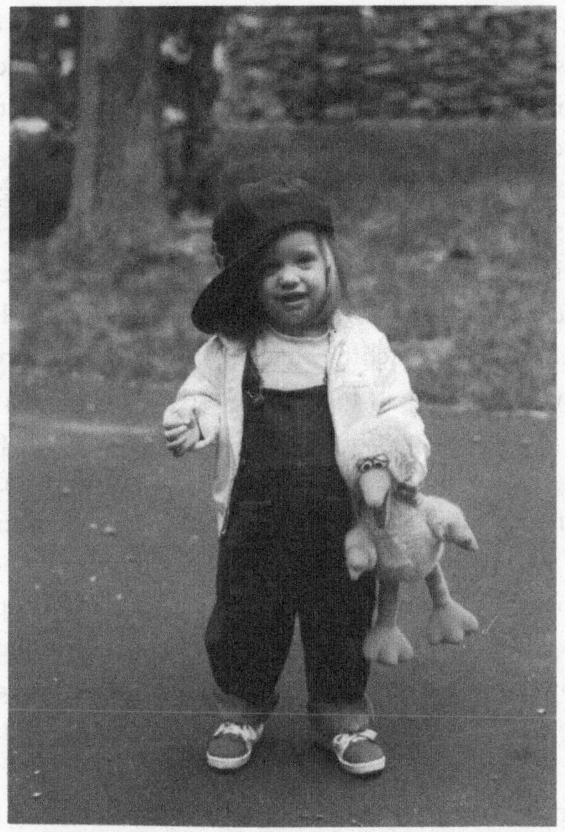

Megan holding her Big Bird toy at two years old.

The First Psychic Reading

If you have never been to a psychic you might wonder what the experience is like. It is not like the seances that are depicted in movies and on television. It is more like a visit with another person, the psychic, who has a message from someone you both know, but whom you haven't spoken with for a while. The psychic can give you the messages that that person wants to convey to you, but has no way of telling you themselves. In my opinion it's almost like receiving a voice mail message from someone you haven't been able to reach for a long time. The psychic is like your answering machine that records a message and makes it possible for you to receive it. It feels good to hear from them again.

In June of 2007 I took my daughter, Sarah, and Megan's friend, Jeanine, to meet with the local professional medium and psychic, Gary McKinstry. This is the same psychic I had seen after my father died. When we met him this time he was having private meetings at a specialty shop a few towns away from us. I had booked an appointment with him in advance. The appointment was booked through the shop with only my telephone number in case of an emergency cancellation. Gary had no way of knowing my name, or any other information about me or why I was there.

On the drive over Sarah, Jeanine, and I had a wonderful talk about Megan and recalled several memories of her. Jeanine recalled the way that Megan was always baking chocolate chip cookies and said that she missed that and missed the aroma of them baking in my house. I used to buy the tubes of cookie dough every week at the grocery store, and Megan would bake several every few days. She loved chocolate chip cookies.

We checked in at the counter of the little shop and we were brought to a porch where Gary was sitting, separated from the rest of the shop and other customers. It was a quiet little area just for us. He greeted us and said that he would be taping the meeting so that I would have a recording of whatever came through. He sat quietly and closed his eyes for a few moments in quiet meditation. I focused on Megan, hoping that would help her to find her way to us. After a few moments, he opened his eyes.

He began by stating that he felt an energy coming through. He felt a pull toward the middle of our group, which was Sarah. The person coming through wanted to know that she was okay. Sarah said that they were probably concerned because she was pregnant at the time.

Gary said, "Did she bake cookies? I'm smelling cookies." He said the presence was very friendly and had a warm attitude. He said that she didn't get to pass at home and wanted to. "She thought she'd someday be the little old lady that would pass at home, but things didn't work the way they were supposed to. Who in the family passed at twenty? She came through to talk about passing at 20–she almost made it to 21. Things are supposed to change in the path–she understands that things aren't what they were supposed to be. She's really keeping tabs on you guys."

Gary said that she showed him the name, Stephen. She said "hi" to Stephen. She didn't get to see him. The morning she died she saw her grandmother, spoke with her father on the phone, and saw me before work, but she didn't see Steve. She wrote his name out for Gary and waved.

Gary asked who was missing today. Megan said that one person was missing. We all figured that she meant her friend Denise, her other closest friend. He said that she was expecting the whole group. Gary asked who the nurse lady was. We told him that must be Megan's friend, Denise. Megan wanted to talk to the nurse and showed him the cap, telling him she's going to get pinned, meaning that she would graduate and be successful.

She wanted to talk about the celebration coming up–a party that she was sad had been canceled. Sarah thought she meant her baby shower. I thought she meant the wedding because we had canceled the arrangements when she died. She said that we have got to bring the family together, "you can't run away, YOU can't run away–you have to have a wedding. Don't elope." Sarah looked at me in shock and said, "You're not eloping!" I explained to her that Steve and I had been talking about eloping because I didn't want to plan a wedding any longer. We had not told anyone about that. Gary continued to say that he was being told by her to have the wedding, "people need to celebrate. She said to bring her picture, I don't care if you're in a church or under a tree, she wants to be there. If you run away there are people who need to be there with you, and she won't be happy about that. She didn't want to screw up your day. She wants to celebrate as a family–she doesn't want things to stop. 'Go forward.'"

She showed snow in April, but a very unusual snow. Sarah said that it snowed in April in Texas while she was there and that it is very rare. We felt that she was trying to make a comment about missing the trip she was supposed to make to Texas in May.

She showed people coming from Rhode Island for her funeral. Steve's sons and many of his friends from the Rhode Island area came to her funeral. "She wants to know about the burial. She wants the closure, she wants a stone with a picture on it dark, dark and shiny" We had her cremated & we hadn't had the interment yet.

She went back to Steve–something special is going on–"He better take care of you or he's in deep shit. She likes what he's doing at home. He's doing it right now. She likes where he's doing it. The dog knew where it should be." Steve was working on the memorial garden when I left the house. He was digging in the area that Snuggles had shown me. "She likes the memorial garden, she loves the tree, but it needs a bench. She loves the spot. She wants water in the garden, she said to get a bird bath" Megan was the only person that knew I wanted to put a bird bath in the yard somewhere.

"An older male is coming through–he's trying to stand up straight –he's wearing a hat, he feels old. He wants to know if the house is still connected to you, is it still in the family, or has it been sold? He's more worried about mom than the house. He's showing oranges–who's in Florida? He's worried about the family in Florida." I think my father wanted to know about the house he and my mom owned. Also, we have a lot of family living in Florida. He wants to say "hi" to the person who bought him the sweater?" I bought him sweaters that we jokingly called Mr. Rogers sweaters. "He feels gentle."

"There's a little lady there too–older. She came through a little on the heavy side–in a dress–a little lost." I wondered if my Memere was trying to come through again.

"She saw Bobby with rocks around him; he drowned in a lake" Had Megan seen my childhood friend, Bobby?

"Why is there a duck pond? She's showing ponds with ducks, evidently, she's home". There are two duck ponds near our house. "She's trying hard to talk to you." I asked if she knows how proud I am of her–"Yeah–She's still connected–when you talk to her, you are *really* talking to her"

She wanted to know how the cheerleader person was. He saw pom-poms and said she is relating to a cheerleader. I wonder if this is a reference to the friend of hers that wrote me a letter referring to Megan as everybody's cheerleader. "Everyone that comes through comes through as very connected"

The following is the summary that came through at the end of the reading:

"If you don't do anything else, have the wedding. This is important, she wants to celebrate, she needs to be celebrated, she doesn't want to feel that things have stopped. So, for everybody's sake, have the celebration, and do the whole nine yards. Party and dance, she'll be there. If you have a DJ, she'll show up in the sound system, she'll make herself known."

"I got the Winnie the Pooh TTFN (Ta Ta For Now). She has things to do. She's pulling back now. Which one got the phone message? She's sorry for the phone message. It's a tough way to find out." Of course, her father is the one who had gotten the phone message but we called Sarah, so she heard over the phone, also.

A Text Message

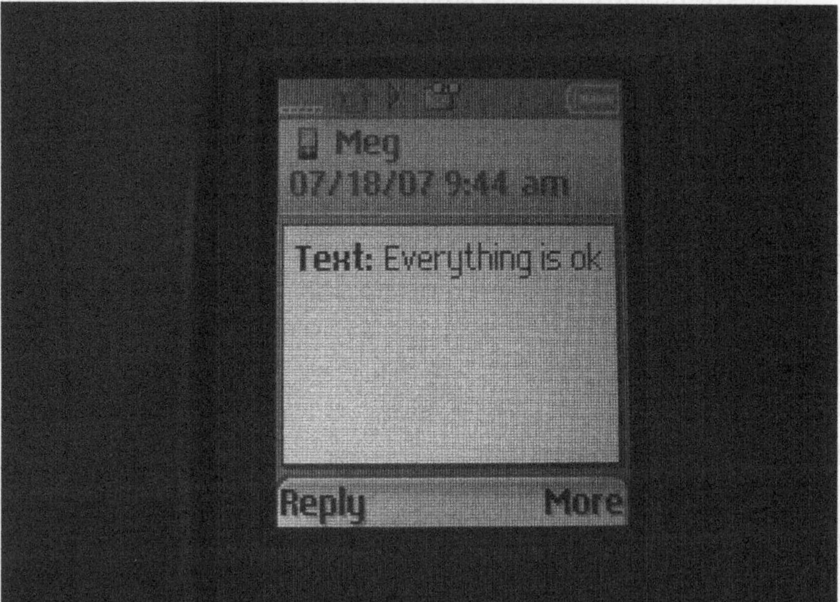

The text message I received from Megan 81 days after she died.

I was at work on the morning of July 18, 2007. I shared an office with two other ladies in the hospital I worked at. I had stepped out of the office for a few moments, and when I returned one of my office mates told me that my cell phone had been buzzing inside my desk drawer while I was gone. Now, this was very strange at the time because I rarely got calls, and my fiancé and I did not have text service at the time. In fact, I had never sent, nor received, a text in my life.

I took my phone out of my purse and saw that it indicated I had received a text message. I had to try to figure out how to retrieve a text because I didn't know how to do so. When I found it, it was from Megan! This was almost three months after she had died! I nearly fell into my chair, and exclaimed that Megan had sent me a text! My co-worker was in shock and asked what it said. I read it to her. It simply said, "Everything is OK". I was shaking from the shock of this. How could this be possible? What could it mean?

Megan's cell phone was never found at the scene of the accident. I knew that her cell phone service was under her father's telephone plan and that he had canceled her service right after the accident. So, it was impossible for anyone to have used her phone to send that text. The phone and the service were no longer in existence. I even called her number to check and got a recording that the number was out of service.

About a half an hour after this happened I received a call on my cell phone. Again, it was strange for me to get calls on my phone. When I answered it, it was the Connecticut State Police. The officer said that he was calling to tell me that they had received the complete accident report and that it had been sent to the insurance company. He wanted me to know that I should be hearing from my insurance company very soon and that this part of the ordeal was over. He said, "I just want you to know that everything is OK". I asked him when he had gotten the report. He replied, "About a half an hour ago".

Could it be a coincidence that the text message I received from Megan came to me about the same time as the accident report was received by the Connecticut State Police? Was she trying to forewarn me? Did she want to be the first to tell me?

This was one of the first real strong signs that came directly from her to me. No psychic; no middle man. Just Megan and me. It was an incredible, pure act of love that crossed the barrier of time, space, life and death. It crossed from the Other side to This side. I didn't know at the time that there would be other times, and other ways, that she would find to express her love and touch me and other loved ones from the other side.

I asked if I could see the car before it was towed away. Once again, I was told that it would probably be too upsetting to me, and the police officer did not think it was a good idea. I didn't care, I needed to see it.

I went to the police barracks again and was let into the back locked area. There it was with a big tarp over it. I asked them to remove the tarp.

I looked through the gaping holes where car windows had been. I saw the broken glass that filled the car. I saw Megan's boots and some bags, CDs, and Planned Parenthood posters. I took everything that I could. I didn't see remnants of blood, which I expected. I guess my funeral director was telling me the truth when he said that she didn't bleed. She had internal injuries. I said a prayer and felt a sense of relief. Somehow, it was sinking in, that she really did not suffer. She simply died.

The experience triggered a more acute awareness of my surroundings than ever before in my life. I wanted to look for signs and be aware of sounds, smells, touches, all sorts of sensations that might be a sign. I wanted to also be leery of coincidences that might seem like signs. I wanted to learn to differentiate reality from wishful thinking. I wanted to see and hear from her, but not act crazy. I learned to open my heart and mind to signs from the Other side, while still remaining in the present reality.

It's a Boy!!

Sarah's baby was due in August. She and I went to birthing classes together at the hospital where she planned to have him. I was excited about being her birthing coach. We had planned a shower for her for July 29, 2007, at the local country club. On July 28th we went to the last birthing class. Sarah told me during the class that she didn't feel well; in fact, she thought she might vomit. We went home and she relaxed the rest of the day. Steve and I had invited some friends over and we swam in the pool, as it was very hot. Sarah went to bed early, saying that she still didn't feel well.

At 4:30 A.M. I awoke to the sound of knocking on my bedroom door. Sarah called to me that she needed to go to the hospital. She had called to report feeling ill all night with stomach cramps and back pain. They had told her to report to the local maternity ward to be assessed. I rushed to put on some clothes and took off with her while Steve followed in his truck. On the way to the hospital, I asked her for more details about what was happening. She had been feeling ill all night and had a bad backache and cramps. As she described this to me I looked at her and said, "You're in labor!" She denied it, stating that it was impossible; she wasn't due yet. I told her that it didn't matter when she was due, the baby was ready!

We got to the hospital about 5:30 in the morning. As soon as she was evaluated, she was told that she was indeed in labor. I guess the baby wanted to be present for his own shower. Now I had to call everyone and cancel the shower that was supposed to begin in a few hours. Alexander was born at 12:08 P.M. and he weighed five pounds, eleven ounces.

Alex and Sarah came home after a couple of days and life with a new baby began in our home. Sarah's husband got leave from the military and came to stay with us, also. Alex wasn't good at eating. He was not getting enough nourishment and began to lose weight. We tried everything to get him to take in more, but nothing seemed to work. Daily weights at the hospital were very discouraging, and Sarah was told that he might need to be admitted to the neonatal intensive care unit in Hartford if he didn't start to eat and gain weight.

Sarah was advised to give him formula a drop at a time with a dropper. We had to get him to take in one ounce each hour, but it was a challenge to get him to consume even one half of that amount. One evening Sarah was holding him and I was on my knees in front of the rocking chair that she was sitting in. I was trying to give him formula with a dropper. I distinctly felt a touch on my head and fingers running through my hair. It was a gentle, loving touch. I turned around to tell Sarah's husband to stop because I didn't want him to touch my hair. He wasn't there. He was in the dining room on the other side of the house!

I knew what I had felt. I looked at Sarah and said, "Alex will be fine. He's going to start eating and get strong and gain weight." She asked me how I knew. I told her I knew because Alex's guardian angel had just sent me a sign that she was watching over him.

He did begin to gain weight after that. I know it might sound corny, but I knew it was a sign from Megan. I knew that if we believed that he would be well, that he would. We believed and he learned to eat and grow to be a strong, healthy boy.

I Carry Your Heart

Some of Megan's ashes were taken by her father to be kept in a small urn. I kept some for myself in a small urn shaped like a silver vase. It actually can hold a few flowers in it. I also had a tiny amount of the ashes put in a teardrop shaped pendant to be kept on a silver chain for myself and a tiny amount in a heart shaped pendant with a silver chain that I gave to Sarah.

On October 27, 2007, exactly 6 months after she died, we held a Memorial and interment of the remainder of the ashes. They were in a pink marble urn. Our family and friends met at the cemetery, and gathered under canopies, while it rained all around us. I was so grateful that many of Megan's close friends were in attendance.

Sarah had found the poem *i carry your heart* by e. e. cummings bookmarked in Megan's favorites. I hadn't known that she had found it and had given her the heart-shaped pendant with Megan's ashes in it the same night. Sarah told the story of this at the interment and then read the poem, all the while holding the pendant in her hand. The line from the poem, "i carry your heart with me (i carry it in my heart)" held a profound meaning in this case.

I got up to speak after Sarah. I quoted a letter that one of her friends had sent to me. She wrote: "Most of all, Megan was everybody's cheerleader. There wasn't anything any of us could do that she didn't support. She was always there to remind us that we're beautiful and intelligent and that we can do anything we set our minds to. She was so proud of all of us, I can't imagine not having that around."

After talking for a short while about Megan I read something I had found that she had written. "To all my beautiful friends: Thank you for making the 'best years of my life' so much more than that. Your open hearts have been a comfort, your senses of humor a diversion from the stress. May you always be this open-minded. Do not become porcelain dolls–beautiful, but empty."

We played a recording of the song, *In My Daughter's Eyes,* sung by Martina McBride. This song has been very meaningful to me because I have learned while raising two daughters that the world looks quite different and beautiful from each of their eyes.

After the service, we all went back home for a small reception. After everyone had left I looked out of my front door. Over the treetops, in the direction of the cemetery, was the biggest rainbow I had ever seen in my life. I heard from people all over the county that they had seen the rainbow and had thought of Megan.

The rainbow that appeared in the sky over the cemetery after the interment of Megan's ashes.

The Angel Dream

About six months after Megan died I had an incredible dream. I dreamt that she came to me and said that I should go to the store and her message for us would be found there. She said the store she liked so much. She said to look for the card with the red bird and I would see her message to us.

When I awoke the dream was so real that I knew it was more than a dream. It was a visitation. I knew she meant a nearby boutique, named Sadie Greene's, that I had often gone to with both Sarah and Megan. We could spend hours looking at all of the unique items in the shop. It is filled to the brim with jewelry, unique cards, scarves, and all sorts of miscellaneous items one would use to accessorize or give for gifts.

Later that day I went to the shop with Steve, Sarah, and Alex. We all set out to find a card with a red bird on it. We thought we were supposed to look at all of the racks of greeting cards that were in the shop. I pictured a card with a cardinal on it and some inspirational message written inside.

I was getting ready to give up after reading every card in the store. I felt very disappointed and sad. Suddenly I heard Sarah say, "Mom, you'd better come over here." I wasn't sure where she was. I found her in a little alcove in the back of the store. I had gone right past it and hadn't noticed the back side of the display in that area.

When I got there, I could not believe what I saw. There were red origami birds hanging from a branch and five other ones in sealed packages in a basket. They were made from a stiff sort of cardstock material; each one a slightly different pattern. The word "BELIEVE" was on the top of the display. There were several things with the word "BELIEVE" on them, such as pins and ornaments. We noticed one ornament with an angel holding a sign which read "Believe in yourself". I took this to mean that Megan was aware of the pink bracelets that had been sold in her memory. Then I saw the most incredible thing–a silver angel pin. The angel had the word "Persevere" engraved on her silver wing.

Megan's message to us was BELIEVE, believe in your selves, and persevere.

I had a tough time holding it together and not crying as we took all of the red origami birds, the angel ornaments, and the silver angel pin to the register. As the saleslady rang up my purchase she said, "Did you find everything you were looking for today?" I said, "Boy, did I ever!"

The Second Psychic Reading

On November 24, 2007, Sarah and I had our second reading by Psychic, Gary McKinstry. Gary started out by acknowledging that he had seen us before.

"I understand the vocal lady with an attitude, but I need to know if she is who you are looking for. Are we still looking for the same person?" We told him, yes, that we were.

"She is complaining about unfinished business. Stuff that was left in the air–it should have been done by now. She understands that it takes a while. The papers need to get filed; things need to get done." I said that I knew she was going to do this. I felt that she was referring to the scholarship. We had not signed the paperwork for it yet. "Who's holding you up?" He said that she wanted us to get it done.

"She's wearing an ugly coat. It looks metallic and shiny. She's shiny and bright. She likes it." It was not what Gary was expecting. "It's very showy, like 'Look at me. I'm the star. I'm here.'"

"Who's the 'C' person?" We thought it referred to a friend of hers. "He has decisions to make." She was giving Gary orders to tell us things, and he said that she was showing us this to tell him that he needs to make the decision. "Get it done. She's very blunt, and not beating around the bush. He has to get over it and do what's right."

Gary asked, "Why is she taking me to a multi-family house? It's a three-family house, a young lady with light colored hair lives there. This is not a relative. What kind of scholarship is this?" I told him it was a memorial scholarship at Eastern. "I'm asking you this because this is the girl who is getting the scholarship. She deserves it. She's not poor but deserves it. She picked her out."

"It's OK to put away her stuff; pack stuff away." I said that every time I go to her room to sort through things I tell her that she needs to help me do this and give me permission to do this. He said that she is giving you permission now. "It's time to pack it up. It's OK to take care of things–she's more concerned with here & now–not the past. She doesn't want any crying–pull it together and move on with life."

"She said that somebody was missing. They found out about her and knew she had died, but didn't show up for the funeral. She couldn't come to the funeral." She wanted to know why. Gary asked what she had done for work because this was a lady older than her connected to what she did. I thought of a teacher she had in school who she later worked for. She was away on vacation and had written a beautiful note to me explaining why she couldn't attend the funeral and sent her sympathy.

"She's showing a little girl. Life has some surprises. There is a connection to a little girl. She will be in the family. This is a prediction."

He went on to say, "I have a really odd question. Have you found the pictures yet? There are pictures that haven't been found yet." I told him that I had found a bag with 20 -30 rolls of film to be developed. "Get them developed. There is stuff on them that needs to be seen. There are good-byes there."

She was standing there quietly for a few minutes.

"I have another really weird question- do you keep the bedroom door shut?" I replied that I had for a while, but now it's open. "She wants it open. Get back to life. Give the stuff away."

Gary changed the subject, "I'm seeing a pickle. It's a Christmas thing." The week before my niece, Debbie, had been up from Florida and we had gone to the Yankee Candle store in Deerfield, MA. Debbie went over to a Christmas tree and asked about the pickle hanging on it. "She was with you there. She's showing the pickle to prove that she was with you at Yankee Candle." She showed him the UMass Amherst area. She started showing him driving up Route 91 in Massachusetts and going to the Yankee Candle shop. She likes Yankee Candle and said to buy a pickle.

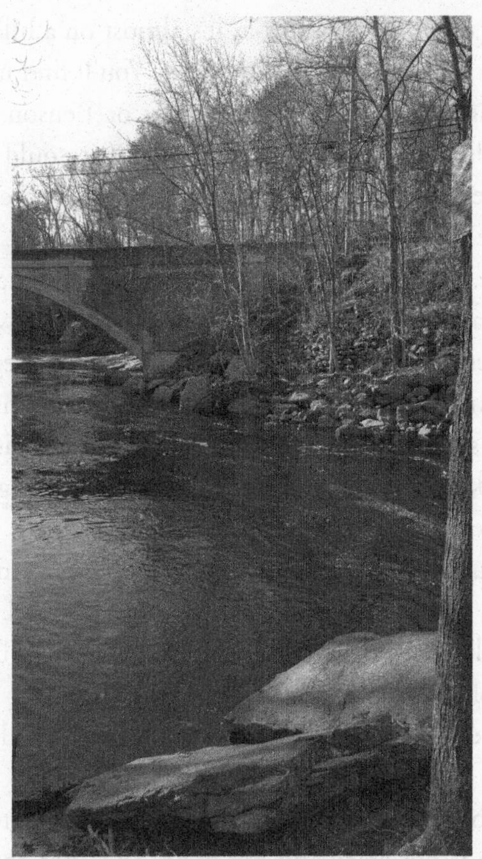

The view of the bridge over Diana's Pool. The accident took place on the road to the right of the bridge.

"Why would she take me to a river? She's going from happy to boom! Super mood. She's showing the water, it looks cold. She's not there, by the way, she's everywhere else. She got very quiet. She literally showed me the river and things got quiet. There's a big guy there–very quiet–he was nice. Have you met anyone else that was there? The guy in the other vehicle has issues. She's upset–she cares about him and how he is doing. She's almost too nice she's the 'advocate lady'. She's worried about the other guy. He needs to know that it's OK."

"The ground is red by the river. There is a monument or some type of marker not far from there. The marker is not for her. It's been there for a long time. If I look for it, it's almost on a hill. I can see the landmark near there. You'll know the spot. You'll find her there."

"She's giving me an odd name–Bently or Benson. Someone she didn't get to talk with or notify." We asked if it could be her friend, whose last name sounds similar to this. She was supposed to go see her that night. "She's worried–is she OK? She feels worried."

"Who is the cheerleader?" This is the second time that a cheerleader was mentioned at a reading. I couldn't help but think it was in reference to the letter her friend had written to me about Megan being the cheerleader. "The cheerleader holds things together. This is what she's doing, whether she knows it or not. She's got a lot of faith in her. She's supposed to pick up the cause–good luck. She has a lot going on in her life, too. But she has got to continue the cause."

He was laughing because she was showing him two novelty Christmas hats. He said that she had bought a comical Christmas hat this year. "It's okay to wear it or use it because she will be there. What does the hat look like?" She had bought a grey baby hat to give to Alex that said: "Where are my presents". He said to have him wear it at Christmas.

"You don't have to let go of her, you know, it's OK to bring her in. The connection is not crazy and not gone. She's not going to let go. I know it was an accident. She hasn't disappeared she will still be there when you get old."

She started showing him Route 84–she was driving down the highway and saying that she had to go down there. "I see girls at school. She associates with girls and relates them to women. There's no sexual orientation intended." We figured as he spoke that she was trying to say something either about the Women's Studies programs that she was involved with, or the Planned Parenthood program with the headquarters in New Haven. "She had a large group of girlfriends. She was very connected to women and girls. There are almost all women around her. She was friends with girls. There is no big "Good-bye" to any boys."

She made several references to the movie "A Christmas Story". She showed him the Christmas Story bunny rabbit suit and other parts of the movie. I said that we were having a Christmas Story gathering at our house that night. She wanted to be there and wanted us to have it so we were having it anyway. "She's glad you're having the party." We had the lamp and the Red Rider BB gun. We played the movie. We even had planned to have Chinese food.

"She's home. She'll be there tonight at the party. She's grinning from ear to ear. She said that we need to celebrate tonight, she's happy for us. She's laughing. Shut the phone off during the party. You don't need the phone, there's a call coming in during the party that you don't need to answer."

Gary was seeing the father from the movie. He asked, "Who's the fried chicken freak?" I told him that we were making chicken wings tonight. Steve wanted to fry them, but I didn't want to. We had had a lengthy discussion about the chicken wings because he insisted they had to be fried. "She said to let him fry the chicken wings." Gary commented, "OK–I'm glad you understand a lot of this."

I asked him if he knows anything about the red bird. He said, "The red bird needs to be by the window. I have one of the red origami birds from Sadie Greene's hung in front of my bedroom window. I told him about the dream.

He asked Sarah, "Why are you headed south?" She explained that she had been in Texas during the summer. Gary stated that he hadn't had someone "checking in" this completely for a long time.

She's again showing the sign for a college in New Haven. "She drove down there. Who's Judy? The Judy she is showing inspired her to social work." We explained that the only Judy we could think of was a social worker at her school and possibly she wanted to be a social worker because of her. Later I realized that there was also a lady that worked at Planned Parenthood in New Haven that might have been the person she meant. He said that she was one of her heroes.

"She's showing tall weeds around and the river. She looks down the hill. I don't know how much more I will get out of her. She's pulling back and fading."

So many messages came through at this reading that it was overwhelming. I knew that she still cared about her friends, especially all of her female friends. She had "chosen" the recipient of her scholarship, and so many other things.

I was very curious about what landmark was right beyond the river and the scene of her accident. I had been down that road many times and had never noticed any landmark.

The most comforting part of the reading was that she was still with us and would remain with us.

Christmas

Megan and Snuggles on Christmas morning, 2006. This was Megan's last Christmas.

I used to love Christmas. I would start playing Christmas carols on Thanksgiving Day. My tree went up that weekend. Everywhere in my home would be decorated with greenery, candles, ornaments, and wreaths. It might have seemed excessive to some, but I loved it and I was very proud of how beautiful it looked.

Christmas is always difficult when we have lost loved ones. The first Christmas after my father died I kept looking toward the empty seat at the dinner table where he used to sit. After dinner was also difficult as we all missed his funny stories and the way he would entertain us and make everyone laugh.

The first Christmas without Megan approached. I felt unbearably sad. I didn't even feel like putting up a tree, but Sarah and Alex were living with us and I didn't want to spoil it for them. Sarah came home with little "Baby's First Christmas" ornaments and I knew I had to get a tree to put them on.

I couldn't bear to even look at the Christmas ornaments. I knew what was in those boxes. They were filled with homemade ornaments from the girls' childhood. There were ornaments with childhood pictures on them. Those boxes held the ghost of Christmas past and I couldn't release it from the boxes.

I couldn't listen to Christmas carols. They all made me cry. My office mates loved to play the radio all day and it felt like a slow torture listening to it. I had to keep asking them to please turn off the radio. Every channel on the television had ads for Christmas and Christmas shows. I felt like I would lose my mind.

I read somewhere that when you are grieving during the holidays that you should still celebrate the holiday, but celebrate it differently than before. Make new traditions. Change it up. I decided to start with the tree. We got a tree, but we did not use any of the old ornaments. I started with the origami birds that I had bought at Sadie Greene's. I added angel ornaments and ornaments that said BELIEVE, HOPE, and LOVE. As I started to tell others of my plans they started giving me ornaments they found in stores and little shops that had an angel or BELIEVE theme. I bought a pickle ornament from Yankee Candle.

It started small and our tree that year did not have a lot of ornaments on it. It had just enough. It's grown since then and developed into quite a lovely tree that celebrates my family more now. The members alive and the members who have crossed over are represented.

At the time of this writing, it has been ten years since Megan died. It wasn't until about three years ago that I could listen to Christmas carols and watch Christmas shows without crying. I am doing alright. I still wish I could feel that thrill and excitement about the holiday, I can't seem to muster that up. Christmas is bearable.

As far as the boxes of older ornaments; I still have never opened those boxes. Every year I tell myself that I will try to open the boxes in another year. Someday I will accomplish that goal, but not until I'm ready and on my terms.

Joshua

Megan, Rebecca, and Joshua at Chuck E. Cheese's
for Megan's fifth birthday party.

My sister, Barbara, was living with my niece, Lisa, and her husband, in Florida. Lisa has two children. Rebecca was one year older than Megan, and Joshua was four months older than Megan. We used to call Rebecca, Joshua, and Megan the Three Musketeers because they were inseparable when they were young. Rebeca and Josh were each living in their own apartments at this time.

On February 21, 2008, just ten months after Megan died. I received a call on my cell phone while at work. It was my sister, Barbara, calling me from Florida. Her first words were, "Susie, Josh is dead!" I was shocked and couldn't figure out what was going on. I left my desk and went out to my car to talk to Barbara privately.

Rebecca had been trying to reach him, but he wasn't answering his phone. She went to his apartment, but he didn't answer the door. She tried calling and could hear his phone ringing from inside the apartment, but he wasn't answering. Rebecca called the police. They broke into his apartment. He was found face down in his bed with a bullet through his head.

The police ruled it a suicide, but none of us believed it. He had been in good spirits the previous evening when he spoke with his girlfriend. He didn't leave a note to help us solve the questions we had. The most compelling piece of information to me was the fact that the bullet had entered his head on the left side and exited through the right ear. Josh was right-handed. I can't imagine how or why a right-handed person would fire a gun with his left hand to commit suicide. There were many unanswered questions.

Once again, our family was torn apart by death. I tried to talk to Lisa about it but she was inconsolable. I understood how she felt. Although Megan didn't die this way, they were both tragic deaths. In the months that followed, I spoke with Lisa several times. I wanted to comfort her, but there really is no comfort except to understand and express love and concern in a case like this. I assured her that I was there for her. I suggested counseling or a support group to her. I also urged her to speak with a reputable psychic. I had found immeasurable comfort in the connection I had with Megan in this manner. Lisa was open to talking with a psychic but was not aware of any in her area of Florida.

Pink Balloons

April 27, 2008, approached. Could it really be one year already? It felt like such a long time since I had hugged her, and yet it felt like just yesterday that she had stood in the kitchen saying "I love you". I decided I had to do something to mark this day.

I planned a brunch for April 27th. I invited family and friends to come to the house. As we gathered that morning we each took a pink balloon and wrote a message to Megan on a small piece of paper. We filled all of the balloons with helium.

We all went out onto the deck in our backyard. A few of us said a few words about how grateful we felt to have the support of so many people through the past year. We played a couple of songs. At 10:27 A.M., the time the first 911 call had come in, we each released a pink balloon with a message in it for Megan in Heaven. After the balloon release, we watched as the balloons drifted skyward.

Suddenly the timer went off on my oven and I ran inside to check it. Everyone outside started yelling for me to get back out on the deck. I was a moment too late! Everyone told me that as the pink balloons got higher in the sky they formed a large letter "M". What an incredible sign! No one was fast enough to get a picture and I had missed it. They said that it was distinctly an "M". Everyone who saw it was blown away by the sight and felt it was a true sign from Megan, to let us know that she had seen us all.

One Year In–One Year Over

I remember thinking that now that it had been one year maybe things would start to feel better. After all, isn't mourning supposed to last for one year? Well, maybe it does in some cases of loss. Sometimes it's even shorter than a year, depending on the relationship with the deceased.

We've all heard about the stages of grief. We all go through denial, anger, bargaining, depression and finally acceptance, right? I mean, that is the textbook answer, right? We've heard about it, read about it, and studied it in school.

Well, it's really not that simple when the death is really personal. In reality, we experience some of these things, maybe all of them, depending on the circumstances. For example, I don't remember ever really experiencing anger. I felt cheated, but not necessarily angry. Maybe I'm splitting hairs here, but it didn't have the same flavor to me.

The first year I definitely felt denial. There are still times when I think of her and I feel the denial that it just isn't possible that this ever happened. It has become a very fleeting feeling now, like a whisper that screams, "NO!!" I think that is why, in retrospect, the first year seemed easier than the second. I didn't know it then, but the second year was when denial stripped away. That's when the real pain started. I could no longer hide my emotions behind denial. The reality was now front and center. It was right there at night when I laid down on my bed and closed my eyes. It was right there, just on the edge, before I opened them in the morning. It was right at the back of my mind and on the tip of my tongue every moment in between. Oh yeah, the second year was harder than the first. It sucked.

My life was interspersed with moments of bargaining. I bargained with God, with myself, and with Megan. I pleaded with God to take me back in time for one more day. I wanted to stand in the kitchen on that morning and hold her. If I only had the chance I would never let her out of my sight again. But we could never live like that, and our children would hate us if we did.

I definitely felt depression. I felt the deepest sadness that I had ever felt. But I was very conflicted in my sadness. In the second year, Steve and I rescheduled our wedding and began making wedding plans once again. I was the saddest I had ever felt in my life, but I was also the happiest I had ever felt. Emotional conflict was an everyday occurrence for me.

I learned that the stages of grief ebb and flow, like the tide. Some days you're happy, some sad. Some days you're frustrated and angry, other days you're bargaining. Emotions don't follow a set pattern, they change, they move, they overlap, and sometimes they let you find moments of serenity. Sometimes a memory, a photo, or a song makes you cry and another day the same thing makes you laugh. I remember feeling at times that I must be losing my mind, but then I would know that I was going to be alright.

People can say the stupidest things when they talk with a grieving parent. For example, someone said to me, "Well, I guess on some level you must feel relieved that your daughter died." I remember being shocked at this comment. I asked her why she would say that. She replied, "Well now you don't have to worry about her anymore. Nothing bad can happen to her." I couldn't comprehend that this person didn't understand that the worst thing that could happen, had happened. She had no comprehension of the reality of my situation.

Another person asked me if I slept at night. I told her that yes, I slept at night. She said that if her child died she wouldn't be able to sleep, and she was surprised that I ever slept. Did she think that she loved her children more than I love mine? I guess that according to her I should never sleep again. What she didn't understand was that the stress I felt every waking minute exhausted me. Sleep was an escape from reality. The tough part was waking during the night and facing reality in the cold darkness of night. It was not being able to fall back to sleep and knowing that I had to face another day without my child. Sleep came in fits and was a temporary comfort only to face the cruelty of waking again.

People say that they understand. They say that they know how it feels. Only another parent that has lost a child can understand. It is insulting and hurtful to a grieving parent to say that you understand if you have not experienced this pain. I would never wish this experience and this pain on any other person, but I resent others who seem to think they understand when they don't.

Meeting new people is always a challenge. They ask how many children you have. Surely, this is not a bad question to ask someone, and I understand it is a common question when you are getting to know someone new. I honestly didn't know how to answer this any longer. It took me a long time to start answering that I have one daughter on Earth and one daughter in Heaven. I feel that this answers the question accurately with the least discomfort for both of us. The problem is that people still get uncomfortable. Sometimes people seem to step back away from me as if my situation is contagious. They don't want to learn more; they don't know how to approach me any longer. In fact, I have had difficulties starting new jobs because as soon as my new co-workers learn that I have lost a child they begin avoiding me. The dilemma is that I refuse to deny the life of my child. Her life had meaning and value. If I don't mention her as being my child I have diminished that value.

Sometimes people tell grieving parents that they should be grateful that they have other children. Believe me when I say that we are eternally grateful that we have other children. We love our living children as much as we ever did. In fact, we might love them even more because we know the reality of the loss.

People might say that the grieving parents are young and can plan for more children. This is a true statement, and I know at least one couple who did have another child and are very happy with their new child. I also know that this does not diminish the pain of losing a child. They still love the one that died, and always will.

People might say that they are in a better place. I speak for a lot of mothers when I say that I will never feel that there is a better place for my child than right here. In the case of Megan, she was extremely happy with her life, her friends, and her family. How could it be better dead?

There are people who don't want to talk about your child. They say that they know it will depress you. It doesn't depress me to talk about my child and other mothers that I know love to talk about their children. Other people are the ones who get depressed talking about our deceased children. It makes them think about their own children's mortality. When we talk about our children it makes us happy because it reminds us and others that they existed, they mattered, and they are remembered.

They will say that you need to "let go", "get over it", and "move on". They say that "Time heals all pain". They are wrong. Time does not heal this pain. None of these things are possible. When you lose a child you never completely let go, get over it, or move on. Life is changed forever. You get to a point around five years after losing a child when you reach an equilibrium. As far as I can tell it is the closest thing to accepting that can be reached. But grieving for a lost child never ends. It only changes. Eventually a new normal will develop in your life.

Keeping Memories Alive

I felt very strongly that I needed to take steps toward keeping the memory of Megan alive. I decided, along with Sarah that we would create the Megan L. Kleczka Memorial Scholarship in her memory at Eastern Connecticut State University. The scholarship was going to be donated each year to a student at the college who was either in the Social Work program, the Women's Studies program or involved with either the Women's Center or Planned Parenthood. I deposited money that had been given to me at the time of her funeral to begin the scholarship.

We had several small fundraisers for it, the bracelet sale provided some funds, and we also held car washes and yard sales to contribute to the cause. We had several thousand dollars in the fund by now, but we had to get the scholarship to at least ten thousand dollars to make it an endowed scholarship. That was the goal. No matter how hard we tried the money just wasn't there. The first year of granting the scholarship approached and we knew that the money would spend down if we couldn't get it to the endowed level.

Around this time Sarah formed a Facebook page to allow family and friends to write about their memories of Megan or to visit to view photos. The name of the page is A Celebration of Megan Kleczka.

In 2008 a group of Megan's friends established the Good News Theatre Group to perform *Godspell* at the Rectory School in Pomfret, CT. A very good friend of Megan's, Paige, organized it, directed it, and starred in it. This group, along with the band members, and a choreographer did an incredible job of bringing the show to life. They memorialized Megan in a very uplifting and spiritual way.

They presented four shows of the production. At the end of the last show on August 24, 2008, I was asked to come up on the stage. I was presented with a check for six thousand dollars to be donated to the Megan L. Kleczka Memorial Scholarship. This was enough money to make the scholarship an endowed fund. I couldn't believe that thanks to all of the young people involved, the goal had been met.

As I accepted the award I looked back at the group of beautiful young people surrounding me and was filled with pure pride and joy. I thanked them and recalled a moment earlier in the week when I went to one of the rehearsals and a reporter had asked me what this production meant to me. I looked at the audience and told about it, and told of my response to the reporter.

"What this means to me is that the scholarship is now an endowed scholarship. That means that it will continue to grow and every year a young person will be awarded this scholarship in memory of Megan. To me, that means that for many years in the future her name will be said and people might ask who she was and why she was important. They may think of why she mattered. And that will keep her memory alive. As a mother who has lost a child, the most important thing to me is that her memory remains alive. That means that she remains alive. And this is what this means to me."

Around then I was contacted by the supervisor of the Planned Parenthood Student Internship program that Megan had been involved with at Eastern, named Gretchen. Gretchen had been an inspiration to Megan, and they had formed a wonderful bond. Gretchen told me that they were dedicating a plaque in memory of Megan in a garden at the Planned Parenthood headquarters in New Haven, Connecticut. She invited us down to the dedication ceremony. Sarah was living in Texas again so she couldn't attend, but Steve and I went, along with some friends of ours. The plaque was engraved with a quote from the letter she had written to apply for the position as a Planned Parenthood Student Intern. I can't express the pride that I felt at her being honored in this way.

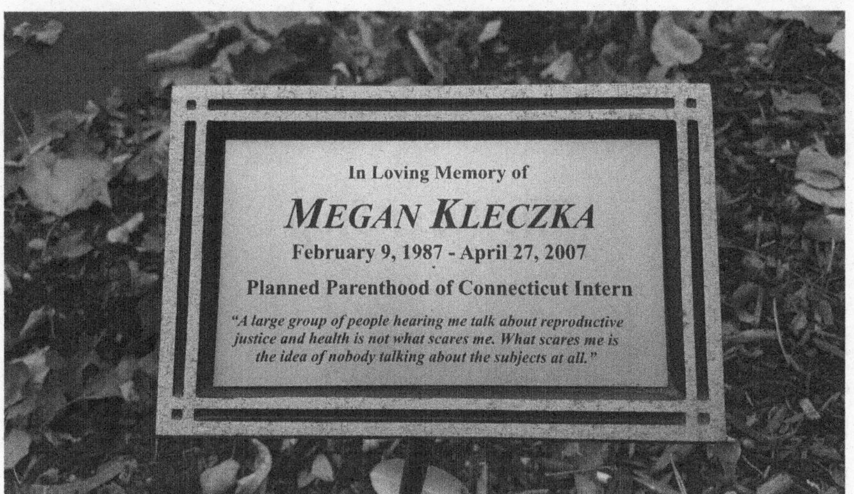

In Loving Memory of
MEGAN KLECZKA
February 9, 1987 - April 27, 2007
Planned Parenthood of Connecticut Intern
"A large group of people hearing me talk about reproductive justice and health is not what scares me. What scares me is the idea of nobody talking about the subjects at all."

The memorial plaque in honor of Megan at the Planned Parenthood of Southern New England Headquarters in New Haven, CT.

When I speak with parents there is a common thread in how we deal with the death of our children. I don't think I have met any parent who has not found some way of memorializing their child. Some parents have found more than one way of doing so. Many parents get a tattoo. Others form a scholarship, start a support group, form a charity, or create a memorial Facebook page.

As a parent I want her name to be spoken, I want to hear the stories about her, I want the memories told and retold. I will never be tired of hearing the funny stories, the sad ones, the touching ones, even the ones that hurt. I think this is how almost all parents feel. So, don't be afraid to mention the children who have passed. Bring a picture you have of them, tell a story, laugh and cry with their parents. Keep them alive in any way you can. We as parents crave this connection, this continuation of our child's life. It validates their time on Earth and our emotions about them when you share them with us. It has never been too long since their passing to talk with their parents about them. Remember, in their parents' heart, they still exist.

The Next Step

I had gone to a therapist during the divorce but had stopped seeing her once it was final because I no longer needed that type of help. I contacted her once again when Megan died because I was distraught. I went to her twice a month that first year. Most of my visits I cried as I told her that I didn't know how to handle the sadness I was experiencing.

After about one year she looked at me and said that she honestly didn't think that she could help me. She had never lost a child and she didn't have anything constructive to say to me. I appreciated her honesty. She said that another client of hers had also lost a child. They were going to a local support group of parents. The name of the group was The Next Step.

I was very nervous about going to the first meeting, but I know that it's always difficult to go to a support group for the first time. I learned later that the group was run by two mothers named Kathy and Chris. They had both lost sons in car accidents about a year before Megan's accident. Some of the parents of the kids who died in the car accident that took place one week before Megan's also belonged to this group.

Kathy looked at me and said, "Welcome to the club that none of us wants to belong to." I introduced myself and told my story. When I got to the point of telling how Megan had died I looked up and I saw tears in the eyes of many of the other parents. In an instant, I knew that they could relate in a way that no one else that I had tried to talk with could.

I finally felt like I fit in somewhere. These parents just got it. We understood each other. I could talk with them. We could laugh and cry together. There was no judgment and no one telling me that in time it would "get better" or that I would "get over" this. We all knew that you don't "get over" losing a child.

From time to time a father would be present at a meeting, but usually, it was just mothers. It might be that fathers grieve differently, or express their grief in a different way. Women talk more and I think, find comfort in talking with other women. Men channel their feelings in other ways.

In the group, we tried a variety of methods to work on our grief. Some of us found relief and peace through yoga and meditation. It seemed to work wonders for some of the mothers and not so much for others. Honestly, I didn't find either method helpful to me.

I began to make a scrapbook of everything that happened when Megan died. I know that sounds morbid, but it really wasn't. I put pictures of her in it with family and friends along with the notes that they had written in cards and messages. I tried to preserve the beauty of the memorials and the uplifting words and thoughts that were expressed. The more I worked on it, the more beauty and peace that came out of it. I found it an exercise in gratitude and love. It also helped me to work through my grief. I learned that to take the things we enjoy and find a way to incorporate them into constructive healing might be the best medicine.

A lot of the parents had been to psychics with varying results and stories. I guess we were all looking for some way to know that our children were alright. We need to know they are safe, happy, and have no pain. This seems to be one of the common threads in the process of grieving.

Around this time, I had gone to a local fall festival with crafts and food booths. I came across a booth where there were several raffles taking place. I approached a man that I saw standing there and asked what the raffles were for. He explained that his three-year-old son had died and he was trying to get money to pass a bill to protect children in the situation that his son had been in. I told him that I was very sorry for his loss and that I could relate because I had also lost a child. He asked how old my daughter was, and I told him that she was twenty years old. He said that I couldn't understand his grief because I had twenty years with my daughter and he only had three with his son. At first, I was taken back by his response.

My response to him was, "I don't know if either of us has more or less grief because of the circumstances. Maybe your grief is deeper than mine because you only had three years with your son. Maybe my grief is deeper than yours because I had twenty years of memories with my daughter. We'll never know the answer because grief is immeasurable. We can't measure it so we can't compare its depth. I only know that we are both experiencing the deepest grief that there is."

We give birth to our children and fall into the deepest love we have ever known; certainly, there is no greater love in life. We feed our children, take care of them when they are sick, protect them from harm, and teach them right from wrong. I struggled with the fact that after trying for twenty years to always protect and guide Megan, I wasn't there at the moment when she needed me the most.

Finally, in The Next Step meetings, I could really talk about grief and begin to sort out those feelings. Through the years we saw a lot of parents in our group. There were lots of children lost due to accidents, illness, suicide, drugs, even murder. You start to feel that you have heard it all. One thing that never changed for me was that every time a new parent came to the group and told their story, they would get to the point where they describe the moment they learned their child had died. Every time they got to that point I felt their emotion, their pain, as my own. You might think that is too much to deal with. You might think that would make me stop going to the meetings. You would be wrong. It's one of the ties that bind us as grieving parents. It's the moment of connection. To me, it's what this group is about. We can't be there when you learn your child died, but we can be there when you have to face that moment again. We know because we have felt that same moment of pure pain.

Parenthood is an all-encompassing responsibility. When it is suddenly ripped from us our hearts ache, our brains can't comprehend, our world is turned upside down. We need to know that we are not alone in this struggle.

There were several topics that arose in the group; some had a common thread with many of us. One such topic was that it seemed many of our children seemed to have either a premonition of death or at least a hint of awareness that death might be imminent. I recalled the times that Megan spoke of death. She said that she would live at home until she died, she wanted to keep Big Bird until she died, Megan said she was going to drive more safely after her friend died. The big indication, of course, was telling her teacher that she wanted to be cremated. I wondered if she knew something, or was just hyper-aware of the fragility of life.

Another possibility is that all children think about death once they are aware of it. I remember as a child thinking about it. I would lie in bed some nights and wonder what it would be like if I never woke in the morning. Would it hurt or would it feel beautiful? Would I see Grandpa again? I think that thoughts of death and curiosity about it are a normal part of learning about life. As grieving parents, we are hyper-sensitive to comments our children may have said.

A Life Interrupted

Megan and her friend, Jen.

On June 14, 2008, Sarah and I took Megan's friend, Jen, with us to meet with Gary McKinstry. The following is a review of the key items he discussed at this meeting.

"Who's the sister?" We asked if he meant Sarah's sister? "Yes. Why would the sister have passed fast? She's saying "Sorry I passed so fast, I shouldn't be gone. There was no time to finish things, no time to correct things."

"Where does the 2- 3 come in? It's a birthday." (It related to Jen's birthday) "Somebody came in and said 2-3. There is a young energy around both of you." Gary indicated both Sarah and Jen.

"Someone is coming through that feels like a mom, not a biological mom, but feels like that kind of energy. A female is worried about you. Who died at 58?" Jen said, "My grandmother died around then.

"The sister is asking about a light. How did someone get her a light? Somebody did something after she passed, it feels like a light or it had something to do with a light. Somebody lit something for her. Where is the sister? Did someone ignite a light near where she is? Maybe it's where she is buried or where her ashes are."

"What's the waterfall? I can see a river, and water, and a bridge. I can see a state park sign. She took me down past a campground and then another campground. There's a sign that says Charlie Brown." There is a Charlie Brown campground on the road where Megan died.

"'I'm worried about somebody else.' She's thinking about someone else that she was worried about. She's telling me that I could go down Route 44 and down Route 198 to get there. That's the way. She's OK, you know."

"Where's the breathing issue? Someone in the family had major breathing issues." Jen said that her grandparents did. "It doesn't feel like a heart problem. It feels like a lung problem." "Why would someone be looking for your dad? There is a message for dad–a male figure that is mad at your dad. Who has what they called a farm?" (Jen's grandfather) "There's a disconnection with the father and son. There was someone around you that went to work and died and never came home. What did your grandfather die from?" Jen said, "We don't really talk about it, but I think it was something sudden." Gary added, "It seems to be something where he went to work and never came home. Your grandparents were nice"

"Who's Eddy? I don't know what Eddy Is supposed to do, but someone wants Eddy to do something."

"The sister is showing flowers. Did someone go to the bridge and throw flowers off of the bridge? She's showing me flowers thrown off the bridge. People have put flowers there.".

"She's talking about New Jersey. She's upset about it." I remembered that Steve and I had gone to Atlantic City and while we were gone she and her current boyfriend had broken up. She had been upset that we weren't home with her when it happened.

"Interestingly enough, she was here now and then. She's a nice girl, but she was scared. Who's the Cathy that she knows? She has reddish blonde hair." We didn't know who he meant by this but acknowledged that she knew a lot of people in school that we had never met. "I'm trying to get away from the water and the bridge. She won't leave there. It feels dark and wet there. I don't understand the accident. It doesn't feel right, the road is wide, and her mind felt very clear. She said she was going east to west. I'm going past the campgrounds and I'm heading down the road, and she said I'm not going the other way, I'm going this way. And it's almost like she doesn't blame anyone. I wasn't drunk or stoned. It feels wet and dismal. It's so beautiful there, but it feels dark. She said that it was a beautiful place to die. The guy in the truck got really messed up. Not physically, but emotionally. She's worried about him. The truck driver wasn't messed up–he was sober. The weather was a contributor, but so was speed, by the way. It's funny, it's like Groundhog Day. She keeps going over it again and again. All she had to do was stop but she didn't. She said, 'All I had to do was stop.' She took me to a place in Pomfret, too. She took me out to lunch. The guy there gave me a big card." Jen said that at the Vanilla Bean Restaurant they give you a big card and pick it up when your food is ready.

She said that we had all gone there, and we were going to sit outside, but we sat in the big room and chatted a lot. "You know she was very comfortable around there." (Meaning our area of Connecticut). "That's where she chose to be. Who's the nurse lady? Say 'hi' to the nurse lady." This was the second time she made a reference to her friend who was in nursing school.

"She's OK, you know? She's not stuck at the accident, but you really need to take a road trip down there, stop at the Vanilla Bean and have lunch. It feels like she'll be with you."

"What is going on in October?" She told him to talk about what is coming up in October. Steve and I had rescheduled our wedding for October. "It feels like it's going to be happy. She said that she's going to be there. She's laughing. She's still pretty. By the way–where you booked it now is fine–she approves."

"What do you want to know? She is not stuck at the bridge. She's not where she showed me. She showed up as the hippy chick at the Vanilla Bean for fun. There's a big dog there, by the way." We had gone there recently and there was a huge dog there.

I said that I wanted to know if she saw balloons. Gary said, "Twice. Somebody else let them go, too." My niece in Florida, Debbie, and my niece in New Hampshire, Darleen, had also released balloons. "She saw them. She didn't miss them and wants you to know. When they get high enough they pop, you know. She wants you to know that. She's still very connected, alive and warm. The fact is that she's gone, but she wants to come back and will keep checking things out."

Gary looked at me and said that even though I was the one getting married that Jen was going to make a nice bride. "You're not getting married now, but you will. You've got some work to do. You think that you will do something else, but she is showing me the wedding dress. You are going to do something traditional."

He looked back at me and said, "Something's up with you. She'll pull a stunt in October. You'll have a surprise."

He asked Jen, "Who married someone for a green card? Somebody you both knew. The guy is going to disappear. It won't work. It's sad, she should have known."

"She said a lot about the scene of the accident." Gary said, "Yeah, there's a reason." I said, "I'm trying to figure out the reason and I'm wondering if she is trying to give me some message about something I'm supposed to do or react to it. The accident report just came out recently. I wonder if she is trying to give me direction as to a way that I am supposed to respond to it."

He said, "First of all, it feels like she is taking responsibility for it. Don't blame the guy in the truck, she hopes he is OK emotionally, too. She keeps showing me the scene and saying that the road is wide enough. It felt wet and she felt like she was moving pretty fast. But again, she takes responsibility for it. She's sorry that she screwed you guys up. But the reason she is showing you the accident is that everyone always wonders what the missing piece is. According to her, she is the missing piece.

The reason she wanted to show it to me, specifically, was so that I would understand the road and I would understand what happened. And I'm the one that has to go there, more than you. Every once in a while, I have to take a road trip. You know where I have to go. Sometime this week I'm going to take a ride down there. She's just sorry, that's all. It's a life interrupted. She's very happy and fulfilled. She lived a very busy life in a short time. And no, I don't think she wants her memory gone, and I don't think it will be."

"Close the gate. She showed an iron gate. I don't understand that one. I have to mention Southbridge. Do you know the really old cemetery next to the performing arts center? It looks like there, but I know she's not there. I see the wall and gate on Main Street." I told him, "That's the cemetery she is in." "She's telling me to close the gate. I'm watching the sun go down, it's really pretty. I can see the sun go down over the hill and I'm watching the light disappear." He said that she looked at him while he was standing there and said to close the gate.

I stated that what I think that means to me is that since we had the interment of the ashes that I have gone back to the cemetery many times and I never, ever feel her there. I feel her at home and all around the house but never there. I feel her presence constantly, but when I go to the cemetery there is nothing there for me. "I think she's trying to tell you to accept the closure. You can close the gate, and you don't need to go there, but she knows that she's not there for you. That's a good thing, and that's what you should do. She's looking to celebrate. Go on with your lives and have fun."

"That's about all I can tell you. You did good. Everybody did good taking care of things. By all means, have her picture at the wedding. You got a surprise picture coming after the wedding, a little paranormal but fun. Enjoy it."

"I do"

We continued with the wedding plans. I really wondered what surprises Megan had in store for us. I felt that Megan had been pretty clear in informing me that she wanted us to have our day and that she would share it with us. I resumed searching for a wedding dress. I was grateful that she had gone wedding gown shopping with me one time before she died. I will never forget her face when I came out of the dressing room with a gown on. Her eyes lit up and she glowed with the excitement of being a part of my wedding. As I began looking for a gown again, I always thought of that moment with each gown I tried on. The search for a gown felt pretty empty and lonely by myself. Sarah was back in Texas with her husband so I shopped alone a lot. My future sister-in-law met me one day to shop. I took Sarah with me as she was home for a visit. That was a fun day, but I didn't find the right gown. Finally, one day, Darleen met me at a bridal shop and helped me search through hundreds of gowns. I knew I wanted something fairly simple, but elegant. After all, this was my second wedding and I was not a young bride. We found the perfect gown and I was happy to finally have that decided.

As all of the plans were made I tried to bring Megan into the plans. I knew if she were still alive she would be involved in every aspect of the planning. I also tried to keep Sarah involved as much as possible from a long distance. Steve and I booked a DJ, photographer, baker, and florist. The service was to be officiated by a dear friend of mine who understood we wanted a non-denominational Christian service. We booked the same country inn that we had reserved the day before Megan died for the April 2008 service. Things were starting to fall into place.

I had already planned most of the guest list the year before. I just had to finalize it. I invited some of Megan's friends who had been to my house a lot as they grew up, and had kept in close contact with me since she had passed. I planned to have them all sit together at the reception.

I wanted to find ways to make sure Megan would be there. We decided to plan a memorial table. We included framed photos of Megan, my father, and Steve's mother. We also framed some of our favorite sayings about our belief in the soul existing after death. The memorial table needed one more special touch. I added the BELIEVE sign from Megan's room. It was perfect and expressed our belief that these three people were still with us.

Steve's twin sons were asked to stand up with him and Sarah was standing up with me. I remembered that Megan had commented once that it was so proportionate that he has two sons and I have two daughters. She had said that it was going to be beautiful to have the wedding so perfectly uniform. This, along with everything in life seemed so out of balance now. As I worked on the seating plan I decided that there would be a seat at the head table for Megan. In place of a plate, her silver urn would sit with her very own floral bouquet to match Sarah's flowers.

We discussed the song we would have our first dance to. There were several songs that held meaning to both of us. However, one song stuck out in my mind. Megan had played it to me one time. She had heard it and thought it sounded like Steve and I. It was *Feels Like Home*, and it was sung by Bonnie Raitt. Steve and I enrolled in dance lessons and learned a choreography to this song. It was perfect.

Gary McKinstry had said that she would be present in the music. Well, the usual wedding reception songs were played. I actually forgot that he had said this. A song came on that didn't fit with the day, and Sarah came rushing over to me saying, "Mom, dance with me. This song is from Megan!" The song was "*Save a Horse; Ride a Cowboy*", one of Megan's favorite funny country songs! Maybe Gary was right about the song; maybe it was just a coincidence. We'll never know, but I prefer to think that Megan sent that song to make us laugh and feel her presence.

The photographer's photos came out very nice, and we picked many of them to put in our album. I didn't find any photos that looked like Megan was in them or had sent any signs through them. There were no "orbs" or mysterious shadows, which I had really hoped to find.

I had bought little disposable cameras and put one on each table, as I had seen done for other weddings and parties. I thought it would be fun to see photos that our guests had taken. A few weeks after the wedding I brought all of the little cameras to the store to get them developed. Photos on the rolls of film ranged from touching to silly. We laughed as we looked at the candid moments our friends had captured at the wedding.

My heart skipped a few beats when I got to the set of photos from the table where Megan's friends had sat. They were full of silly pictures of them. The background of the photos was filled with various sized pink blurs, streaks, and blobs. It was like someone threw pink paint on the background. She was all around them. It was as though Megan had been partying with them all day! Then I saw one of the pictures that had been taken on that camera by one of her friends. It was blurry, but it was me on the dance floor. My dress showed white, but there was a streak of pink running through it. Was Megan dancing with me? I like to think that it was taken during "*Save a Horse, Ride a Cowboy*", but I don't know that as a fact. I know that it can never be proven, and I know there is no answer. I just choose to believe. I do.

Baby Powder

Steve and I went on another Caribbean cruise for our honeymoon. While we were in the Bahamas our ship docked on the cruise line's private island called Half Moon Cay. I had been to the same beach on the two previous cruises that I had taken, also. Every time that I went there I was amazed at how beautiful it is. The water is the perfect turquoise blue and the perfect temperature to swim in.

There is a little chapel on the beach where people have held destination weddings. There is also a bar on the beach called "I Wish I Could Stay Here Forever". I can't imagine anyone has ever gone to that beach and did not felt exactly that sentiment.

While Steve and I sat on the beach I picked up a handful of the sand and slowly let it sift through my fingers. I looked at Steve and said, "I have never felt sand so incredibly soft. This sand is so soft that it feels like baby powder running through my fingers. It's incredible." Steve kind of laughed at me and teased me about the sand. I made him take a handful and let it run through his fingers. He finally admitted that it felt really soft. We both laughed about it.

As I sat there breathing in the beauty and just absorbing the wonder of a place like this in the world, my mind wandered to thinking about Megan. She loved beaches, and she wanted to travel. She wanted to go to Italy the most and was determined to go there in her lifetime. I wondered if her spirit had gone there now that she could be anywhere that she wanted to be. I wondered if she had ever seen Half Moon Cay. I hoped she had.

A Group Visit

In February 2009, four months after the wedding, my hairdresser held a group psychic meeting at her hair salon. When she invited me, she informed me that Gary McKinstry would be there. There were about ten people present as we all gathered in the seating area in the salon. When he arrived, he recognized me from my past meetings with him. I wondered if Megan would have anything new to say to me.

He began conducting readings at the other side of the room. As always, when you attend a group meeting like this, not everyone gets a reading. It's kind of a gamble. You pay your money and you hope you hit the jackpot. Some of the readings were phenomenal, and almost everyone had a reading.

I was one of the last ones to get a reading. Then he turned to me and said, "I'm not sure what I can tell you that I haven't already said." He was quiet for a few moments and then he said, "She's talking about a picture that you brought to the wedding. You did a good job. You did what you were supposed to do. The candle had to be relit. I don't understand this, but she's saying that a candle had to be relit." There were candles on all of the tables. One of the people at the wedding kept blowing out the candle at their table. "She saw the pictures you brought to the wedding. It felt very upbeat". She must have seen the memorial table.

"She's got sand in her toes. It's a happy feeling. Are you the one that told her about the powdered stuff. She was listening. She was at the beach with you when the sand felt like powder. The main thing is that you were supposed to have a good time and you did." I was really shocked. Of all of the things that he had said to me, this one was the most magical; it proved an absolute connection. Megan was at Half Moon Cay with us!

"Everybody was happy. A song came on that wasn't supposed to be there. She did a couple of funny things that day. She was dancing and having a ball."

"Now she's at a beach with courser sand. There's a long stretch of beach and I can see the rocks. It looks like Maine. The clouds are out, but it's still a nice day. She's just walking down the beach. If you ever want to connect with her, here is a little secret. Before you go to bed, envision the beach. Like a big horseshoe bay, and way down the other end, she's there. Let her walk up to you. Just relax and let her approach you. She will come to you really strong." I said that she comes to me in my dreams. He said, "I know, but you have to figure out how to get to where she is. If it helps, count down from ten until you see the beach."

Tattoo Me

My tattoo in honor of Megan.

I never had a tattoo. I entertained the idea of getting one for a while once when I was dating a man that had a lot of them. He had taken me to a tattoo parlor and I had watched him getting one of his. I thought it was really interesting to watch. I even gave some thought to what type I might get. I thought I might get something celestial looking. The moon and stars might look cool. I stopped seeing him after a short time and forgot about getting one.

After Megan died I started thinking about getting one again. It had to be something that reflected the feelings I was experiencing. I believe that every tattoo has a meaning, and everyone with one had a reason for getting it. We talked about tattoos in The Next Step. I was surprised at how many of the mothers had gotten a tattoo in memory of their child.

One day I was cleaning out some things and I came across a card Megan had given to me. I looked at the beautiful words she had written and then her signature. It said, "Love you, Megan". Isn't it strange how the signature of someone who has died can bring that person back to you? It's uniquely their mark. I remembered a card Jeanine had shown me that Megan had signed with a tiny heart after her name. I called Jeanine and asked her if she could bring that card to me. Could I borrow it from her?

I decided to take the signature from my card and the heart from Jeanine's card. I took out the word "you". I had the tattoo that would be perfect. Megan's signature, "Love, Megan" with the tiny pink heart she had drawn.

A friend of mine had told me about an excellent tattoo parlor near us. I brought the cards in and showed the artist what I wanted. I knew that he was well known and had done some incredibly elaborate and artistic tattoos. He looked at me when he heard me say that this was my daughter's signature. He said, "Well, then I know that this is a very important and special tattoo. I need to do a really good job on this one." I wanted to cry because he understood the significance and value this held.

Steve thought I would be in pain, but to me, it felt comforting. I couldn't stop smiling as the needle tattooed my leg with the sign of Megan. Finally, a tattoo as unique as her, as unique as the tattoo she left on my heart.

Puddles

From the time that I bought my house, there were three puddles that would always form in the driveway in the spring, and sometimes other times of the year when it rained heavily. Two of them were medium-sized and one was very large. Sometimes these puddles would get quite deep and maybe be as deep as six inches. The frogs and toads in the yard loved them and could often be seen in them.

When Steve moved in with me he was continually bothered by the puddles and was determined to level the ground thereby eliminating them. He named them Puddle Sarah, Puddle Megan, and Lake Sue as a joke. He brought in equipment to level the ground and had gravel delivered to fill it in. The puddles subsided for a time, but would still resurface now and then.

When Alex was about two years old the puddles became filled with water again and got very wide and very deep. Just for fun, I brought Alex out with his rubber boots on. I encouraged him to jump in the puddles and splash. He was having a blast, laughing and squealing. I was laughing because it was so silly to watch the pure joy he was filled with. I felt so happy and knew that Alex was one of the few purely joyful things in my world. I remember thinking that Megan would love to be here playing with him.

A couple of months later my friends made an appointment for a private reading with Gary McKinstry. After their meeting, I asked them how it went. Did they have a good reading? They said that they had an awesome meeting. They told me a few of the things that had been mentioned. Then they told me that they had a surprise visitor at the reading. Megan showed up briefly. They knew it was her by the description and circumstances.

They said that she had a strange thing to say. She said that she saw the little boy playing in the puddles with boots on. She thought it looked like fun and she wished she could play with him. She said that if she could, she would get boots and splash with him!

The Weekend Megan Came Home

One summer weekend I was just puttering around the house; cleaning and doing the laundry and the usual Saturday household chores. Little did I know that this particular weekend would be remembered as the weekend that Megan came home.

I went upstairs with a laundry basket of clean clothes to fold and placed the basket on my bed. I saw one of the pink "Megan bracelets" on the top of my bed. I didn't know where it had come from, as I hadn't worn one for quite some time, and I hadn't seen them around the house lately. I picked it up, put it on my wrist, looked around, and said, "Hi, Megan, I'm so happy to have you home today." Then I continued with my chores.

Later that evening my husband and I were sitting around the campfire in our backyard with our neighbors, their son, and their daughter, who had been a close friend of Megan's. She went into the house for a moment. When she came out again, she was teary-eyed, saying that she thought she smelled Megan's perfume in the house, and it made her miss her very much. I told her that she probably did smell it; that Megan had visited earlier in the day, and maybe was still with us.

The next day Alex was playing in the house while I cooked and cleaned some more. I latched the hook on the front screen door so that he couldn't go out in the front yard, as it would be dangerous for him to go near our busy road. Later in the afternoon, I heard the screen door slam. I ran to the door in time to see Alex run down the front steps. I ran after him, calling to him to stop, but he didn't stop. When I caught up with him I grabbed his arm so he wouldn't run close to the road. He looked sad and waved toward the sky. He said, "Bye-bye." I asked him who he was waving to. Now, Alex was severely speech delayed and at this point in his life he was still in speech therapy and did not have strong language skills. He had not been speaking very many words and not many that were really clear at this point. He looked at me and said, "Aunty Megan." He looked back to the same area where he had waved, got a big smile, and waved again. He said, "Bye-bye, Aunty Megan". Then he turned to me and took my hand and walked back to the house with me. I asked him if he had played with Aunty Megan, and he nodded an affirmation. I asked him if she had to leave and he said, "Yes". I guess that it was time for her to go. I turned around, and waved, and said, "Bye-bye, Megan, come back to visit again."

The Bubble Dream

I had another dream about Megan. It was one of those dreams that seem so real that when you wake up you feel like it was real and the state you are in now is questionable.

In my dream, I was climbing up and then I was in an open elevator going toward the sky. I climbed higher and higher. The elevator stopped at a beautiful place and I stepped off the open elevator onto a ground that was all pink. There were pink bubbles all around that reflected all of the colors of the rainbow. It was breathtakingly beautiful. I saw a beautiful female angel coming toward me. As she got closer I realized it was Megan. She was surrounded by bubbles. I felt tears falling from my eyes, but still had the biggest smile I thought I had ever smiled. My heart was filled with pure joy. She smiled back at me and said "Hello, Mom. I love you." I told her how much I loved her and missed her. I reached out to touch her, to hold her. She told me to stop. She said that in this place everything was beautiful, perfect in fact, but that she couldn't touch me, and that I couldn't touch her. She said that she had to go, but she wanted me to know that she was fine and happy. And then she faded away.

I awoke and felt so blessed to have been given a glimpse of what might be. It is said that dreaming of bubbles may mean hope and a belief that good, positive things are possible. I choose to believe that Heaven is what we as individuals see as perfection. In other words, that each of us has his or her own Heaven. It is where we are finally at Peace with ourselves and others. I saw Heaven in this dream as a place of beautiful bubbles, a good place where Megan exists and positive things are possible. Maybe Heaven is different for all of us; maybe it is what we, as individuals, perceive as paradise.

I also think that the concept of not being able to touch each other is reminiscent of the dragonfly story. The dragonfly can see the ones left behind and appreciates their existence, but can never return and touch them. Just as there is water that comes between the dragonfly and the larvae, there is a space that cannot be crossed between us on Earth, and our loved ones on the other side. Maybe our loved ones are really just beyond our reach, but close enough to watch over us.

It reminds me of something I heard once from a psychic. He said that there is a way to explain death to children, but I believe this is relevant to all of us. He used the example of the simple science experiment we learned in grammar school. Take a glass of water and mark the level of water in the glass. Wait a week or so and look at the glass again. Notice how much less water is in the glass now due to evaporation. Those water molecules are still here, but they have taken on a new form. They are now moisture in the air around us. They are still a part of our existence as we live and breathe. We can't see them, touch them, or smell them. Well, when the people we love cross over their soul, their essence remains. It is all around us, but we can't see them or touch them. They are but particles in the space surrounding us. As I see signs and feel the presence of my loved ones I choose to find comfort in this concept.

A Home Visit

I scheduled a group reading with Gary at my house on November 21, 2009. Some of my friends, a few of Megan's friends, and of course, Sarah, attended the reading. Gary tapes his meetings, but several other attendees taped it also, including me. At the end when we tried to play back the tapes none of them came out well. The sound was very muted and muffled. Gary said that he felt that there were mischievous forces interrupting it. I told him the story of what we always called "the ghost in the house".

Through the years we have had strange occurrences take place. Sometimes items go missing and after searching everywhere I will finally tell the ghosts to bring it back. I often find it right after that in a spot that I had already searched to no avail. Gary agreed that there was more than one spirit residing in my home, but they were harmless souls.

There were several readings that day. My neighbor's father-in-law came through. He told his son to buy a safety rope. His son had recently cut down a tree that had hit their house. Everything he said was very funny because it was so relevant.

The mother of a friend from work also came through. She had died decades prior to this, and her daughter was very grateful to hear from her mother after all those years.

He asked who the young person who passed fast was. She was coming through as "spicy". He said that there is a picture of her in boots. We all thought it was a certain picture of Megan in a Halloween costume. He said that he loves her sense of humor. He doesn't understand her showing a volleyball game. He said they are someplace outside and playing volleyball. Everyone is having fun; like on a beach.

He was looking at letters and her message went deeper. He had trouble understanding this at first. She said that it meant something and is important; it was unfinished. The writing is about a subject, not just friendship letters. It was started and needs to be finished. It's something she felt strongly about. We all agreed that we thought this was in reference to the work she was doing with Planned Parenthood. He said that he keeps going from serious business to fun and funny feelings. We explained that that is what Megan was like. She was very serious about her work with LGBT issues, women's health and women's rights, and equality, but at the same time, she was funny and nutty about life, family, and her friends.

Gary asked who the person was who had gone to Mexico. I looked at Megan's friend, Paige, who had gone to Mexico with their friend, Denise, a couple of weeks after Megan died. They had felt a bit guilty about going so soon after she died, but the trip had been scheduled long before. Gary said that she was there with them. She wanted them to celebrate; she didn't want anyone feeling morbid or sad. Now it's time to go forward. He said that there were strawberry daiquiris. Paige said that was what they drank the whole vacation. He went on to describe a scene where a good-looking bartender had pulled out a machete to chop a pineapple for their drinks. He also told the story of them each wearing toe rings and one of the rings was lost on the beach. Paige was shocked and described the scene with the bartender and the machete. She went on to say that they had both bought toe rings and hers was lost on the beach. Gary said that Megan was with them in Mexico. He said, "By the way, why do we go into so much detail about these things? It's because she wants you to know that she was really there with you." Gary said that Megan was laughing because she was so happy to be with us.

He spoke with Megan's friend, Jeanine, and a boy Jeanine knew that had recently died came through. He said that he was a young man with too much stress. He valued his friends like family. Her mother was sitting with Jeanine and Gary started to have a man come through who had had a heart attack. Then Jeanine's father came through wearing khakis, which is what he always wore. The number forty-six came through and he was forty-six when he died. They had several connections that all made sense to them.

While he was reading the first young man he started to say that another young man wanted to send a message to Rebecca, not Becky, but Rebecca. I said that I thought that was for me. I was thinking of my nephew, Joshua, who had died the year before. His sister always insisted that everyone had to call her Rebecca, she didn't like to be called Becky. He said that he couldn't call it murder, but it was pretty close. Some people thought it was a suicide, but Gary said, "There was another guy in the room. It felt like there was a struggle. He's okay now. Even after the shot the person never called. He could have called 911, but he didn't. The other thing that was odd is that he was in an upright position. It seems weird because the position he was in doesn't line up with the gunshot he received. In other words, they called it a suicide to get it off the books. The other guy with him knew. It wasn't over money. That is the best that I can tell you."

During a break in the visit, Gary went out on the front porch for a few moments. When he came back in, and before he began readings again, I asked him if he would like to see a photo of Megan. He looked at it and then looked at me and told me that it is exactly as he pictured her when she comes through.

Another Psychic

Sarah and I went to see another psychic who held a group meeting in a nearby town. There were about fifty people in the room. She made her way around the room connecting with a variety of people. I was hoping that Megan would come through, but as the evening passed I began to give up hope that I would get a message.

She started to say that she had a World War II veteran coming in. The more she said about him, the more he sounded like my father. Sarah and I looked at each other and both realized this about the same time. We acknowledged that we thought the reading was for us. There were things she said that made sense and some that didn't. Then she said that she hoped I wouldn't be offended by what she was about to say. She said that he was laughing about the mushrooms. I was really confused now. She said that he was watching two men as they were looking at mushrooms growing in the yard. One of the men thought the mushrooms looked like penises and the mushrooms smelled terrible. He was laughing at the two of them because they were so funny. I was baffled because now I really had no idea what she was talking about.

We went home and told Steve about the reading. He was shocked and told me that he had been next door on the weekend and our neighbor had shown him some strange mushrooms that were growing in his yard. They looked like penises and when they kicked them they gave off a horrible smell. The two of them had been laughing about the mushrooms. Apparently, my father was with them at the time and was laughing along with them.

Snuggles, Part 2

After Megan died Snuggles' health really declined. She was getting old and she definitely missed Megan. We tried all kinds of foods to get her to eat better. We even started cooking chicken and grinding it for her. We would serve it to her after mixing it with rice. She kept losing weight. She became very frail and sickly. After spending thousands of dollars on her veterinarian expenses with no improvement in her health Steve looked at me one day and said, "Poor Snuggles has no quality of life left. It's time, Sue. We have to help her." We brought her to the vet one last time. We told her how much we loved her and held her as she passed. It was one of the hardest things I have had to do. She was a good dog. We instructed the vet to have her cremated. We got a call about a week later to pick up her ashes. Steve picked them up on a Friday on his way home from work and placed the container of them on the mantle, next to the vase that holds Megan's ashes.

That Sunday Sarah commented, "I feel Megan's spirit so strongly this whole weekend. Why do you think that is? What's different?" I was so amazed that Sarah had felt something. Sarah hadn't realized that Steve had brought Snuggles' ashes home on Friday. I replied, "Snuggles came home, and is with her. I think they are happy."

An Embrace from Dad

My mother needed more help as she aged in her home. My father and Eddy were gone, and I was her primary caregiver. I was determined that I would stay true to my promise to her. I would take care of her until the day she died. I took her to the grocery store and doctor appointments. I paid her bills for her and balanced her checkbook. I prepared some meals for her and made sure she had all of the necessary food and medications. I set up her medication box each week. I even scheduled home repairs and maintenance needs. Steve mowed her lawn, shoveled her driveway and walks in the winter, and repaired everything that broke or needed upkeep. Sarah helped with everything she could and watched over her whenever we were out of town. It was a daily commitment, but it was done without reservation. We took care of her out of love with the goal of keeping her safe in her own home.

At one point she needed to have a medical procedure at the local hospital. Her doctor told me that I would need to sleep at her house the night prior to the procedure to make sure she was safe during the preparation for it. I went to her house after work and helped her with the preparations.

She went to bed around ten o'clock at night and I got comfortable and ready to sleep on the couch in her living room. I was laying there and felt almost ready to drift off to sleep when I thought that I heard something from the kitchen, which was next to the living room. I didn't even open my eyes because I thought it must be nothing. Then I could swear that I heard my father clear his voice the way that he often had. A moment later it felt as though something or someone was around me in a warm and comforting hug. It was like a blanket of comfort embracing me. I thought I could smell my father's aftershave. I heard him in my mind saying "thank you for taking care of her, keep up the good work." Of course, there weren't words spoken aloud. It was more a communication that came to me.

I puzzled, wondering how this sort of thing, this feeling, could occur. I certainly did not feel a physical hug. It was more like an emotional embrace. I wondered if it was just my imagination playing tricks on me. But then, the feeling I had was very real. I felt as though my father was right there, reassuring me. I knew that if he was anywhere on Earth, it would be with my mother. He had been dedicated to her for over fifty years. I remember my mother melting in tears after he died when she looked through his wallet. She had never gone through it before, as she believed in respecting the privacy of others. She found a photo of herself in his wallet. It was taken in 1949, on their honeymoon. He had carried it in his wallet for over fifty years.

I believe that he watched over her from the other side, as well.

Salem

My husband and I like to go away for a weekend in October to Salem, MA sometimes. Yes, *the* Salem, MA, the place where the Salem Witch trials took place. The whole town is like a festival at that time of year. There are street vendors and all sorts of activities. People dress up in all sorts of costumes and some even role play. In fact, we have been known to be in costume, also. It's a really fun time. I like to go to some of the psychic fairs and see if a message will come through for me. Most of the time there are no real messages.

One time I paid for a psychic and waited my turn. I was told to go to a table where there was a young man sitting. He fumbled with some tarot cards and started to make things up as he went along. It all sounded very bogus. I told him that I thought he was a fake and I wanted my money back. He was upset, but brought me up to the main desk and asked them if they would refund my money. The lady at the desk was upset and proceeded to tell him off. She said that she was sick of complaints about him and if he couldn't do his job he should get out. I felt bad for him, but there really is no room for fakes. She couldn't refund my money, but she sent me to a different psychic.

I sat down across from the lady I was sent to. She looked at me and said that she was supposed to read tarot cards, but she wasn't going to do that with me. She said that I had a spirit around me. She shut her eyes as her face scrunched up tight. The psychic immediately said that she was being shown April and that the side of her head hurt, as she held the right side of her head. It hurt on the side of her neck, mouth, and head. She opened her eyes and looked straight at me and said, "I died." She said that it happened in April, but she's OK now. She went on to say that she saw a grave stone or marker and that Megan likes the writing on it and how it's worded. I had been trying to make a decision about the purchase of a gravestone for the cemetery. I was unsure of what I wanted to get but had one idea in mind.

She saw a picture of a little girl in a white dress. I think she meant a picture I have of Megan playing dress-up. She went on to say that I had three children, the middle one was not born, and the light-haired one had died. This was the third psychic to read that I had three children.

The psychic saw a radio and said that music stations were changing back and forth. She said she communicates with me through music. She saw Sherry Lewis and Lambchop singing "*This is the Song That Never Ends*", which is a song Megan and I used to sing together and watch on video when she was little.

Megan was worried about her grandmother, my mother. The psychic went on to speak of a pond near the accident site, and said that it is pretty there. I believe she was referring to the area named Diana's Pool, which is under the bridge where the accident happened.

Megan is happy about things that have been published about her since she died. She's very proud & never thought she would get such recognition. She said I would get an amethyst soon and Megan would be instrumental in me finding it. The first thing I saw was an amethyst in the next shop that I went into.

She started talking about the little dog who had died; saying that she was close to my daughter that was on the other side, and now they are together. They are happy and comfort each other. She saw them playing together.

She admitted that she had a lot more to say, but had to stop because our time was through.

Send Me a Sign

Another anniversary rolled around. Could it really be seven years already? I had taken every anniversary and all of Megan's birthdays off of work so far and had decided that I always will. I am just too upset on those days. I started to feel that if I can keep up with life 363 days out of the year that I deserve to let myself grieve on those two days. This time the anniversary fell on a Sunday so I didn't have the need to request time off.

Steve asked me to go to one of the Rhode Island beaches with him so that I could get out of the house. We drove down and I put a message in a pink balloon. This is another annual ritual that I have done every year on the anniversary. I stood on the beach and released the balloon. I asked for a sign that she was still around me. I just wanted to see or feel something from her again.

We drove along the coast, taking in the sights of the ocean and the shore. After a while, Steve said that there was a place he wanted to show me. It's called the Umbrella Factory, but they don't make umbrellas there! He pulled off of the road and into a small parking lot. We walked through a wooded area and came upon a couple of buildings. They had crafts for sale and a wide variety of small shops. One building had a sign for a second-floor shop that seemed intriguing to me so I suggested that we go up there. It turned out to be a consignment shop for crafters. The first counter that I walked up to had beautiful and unique pendants that the crafter had handmade. One caught my eye. It was a beautiful shade of teal blue with an off-white colored dragonfly. I picked it up and immediately loved it. I turned it over and saw the price–a little too steep for me to spend on one pendant. I went on and looked at all of the other tables and booths in the shop. I kept getting drawn back to that pendant. I just couldn't get it out of my mind. I must have gone back to it about six times.

Meanwhile, Steve had been walking around, admiring various items in the shop. He walked up to me and asked if I had seen anything interesting. I showed him the pendant. He thought it was pretty cool looking. I took another walk through the shop. When I came back to the front desk I found Steve chatting with the sales clerk about the shop and the crafters who rent space in there.

We left and headed back to the car, but we had to hurry because it was starting to rain lightly. Steve started the car, but when he went in reverse he stopped suddenly and put it back in park. I looked at him, wondering what was wrong. He said that he was hoping to wait until Mother's Day, but he couldn't. He had something that was "vibrating in his pocket". He reached in and pulled out the dragonfly pendant. He had bought it to give to me on Mother's Day in two weeks. He said that as soon as he got in the car he felt like it was vibrating and he knew he had to give it to me right then. I felt like this was my sign from Megan on her anniversary.

I couldn't wait to get home and find some beads that I could use to make a necklace with it. I started pulling out all of my beads, but none of them seemed right. The color was off or something just didn't seem to work right. My creative side was really feeling frustrated because I couldn't find the right beads to compliment it. Then I opened one last container of beads, one that I usually didn't consider because those were odd beads that didn't seem to go with any of my usual projects. Suddenly I saw them. The blue and off-white colored sea glass. The souvenir from the day Megan and I went to Provincetown on Cape Cod. I had told her that someday the right thing would come along and they would be perfect. That day had come, almost ten years later.

I started working on the necklace with the beads and a piece of silver chain. I found all of the right components to make the necklace perfect. I even had enough sea glass to make earrings. It was finished in a little over an hour. It is one of my most treasured creations because Megan was such a huge part of it.

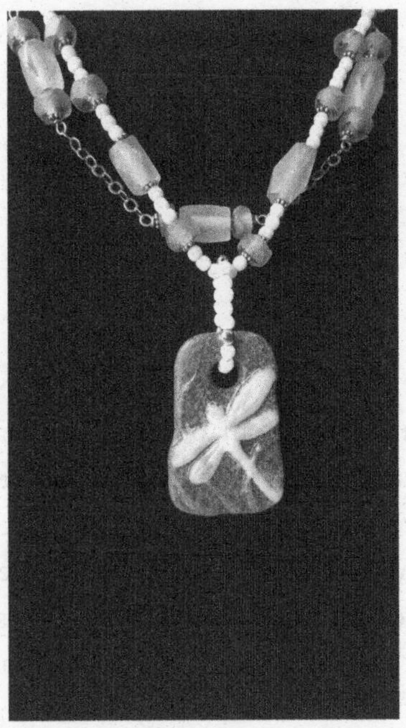

The necklace I made with the dragonfly pendant we felt Megan had sent to me and the beads I bought on our day in Provincetown.

That summer the backyard seemed filled with dragonflies every time I went out there. They would fly around and land on me. Sometimes they just sat on my finger or on my chest for almost an hour. Every time that happened I would say, "Hello, Megan. I love you."

Bermuda

We decided to take a cruise to Bermuda out of New York. This was different for us because all of our other cruises had been out of Fort Lauderdale. We went through a terrible storm at sea on the way to Bermuda. Almost everyone on the ship was seasick. We were fortunate to be some of the few people who were not affected by the storm and high seas. I had never seen anything like it. The ship was rocking so hard that the indoor pool had to be closed off because waves in it were sloshing all over the deck and it was dangerous to walk in that area. The outer decks were closed because it would be too dangerous to go there also, and there was a fear of someone going overboard.

As we approached the islands of Bermuda the seas calmed and people began coming out of their cabins. The island was beautiful, the water was a beautiful shade of blue and the skies were finally clear and crisp. We were trying to decide which beach we would go to, as Bermuda has incredibly gorgeous beaches. The first day there I ended up with a sunburn even though I used sunscreen, and nothing seemed to soothe it. We figured this was going to put a damper on the beach as we had to make plans that did not include going to the beach.

We decided to book a shore excursion on a boat to an isolated cove where we would have the opportunity to do some sea kayaking. This seemed like a fun adventure that would substitute for laying on the beach. We were brought to a cove on the far end of one of the islands. We were told that we were on the tip of the Bermuda Triangle. It was absolutely beautiful! We got in our kayaks and set out on the water to see a sunken ship. The water was so clear that we could see right down to the shipwreck as it lay under the water. Fish were swimming all around it and going in and out of it as we watched. The tour guide then directed us to another cove and we started to see a beautiful little beach that was tucked away. We were kayaking to the beach. We pulled up and brought our kayaks up on the beach and took a walk through a salt marsh to see some of the local birds and vegetation.

After we got back to the beach we were able to swim a little and just enjoy the moment. I sat on the beach and I thought about Megan, as I do every day. I thought that she would love this beach. I wondered if she was there with us just as she had been at Half Moon Cay. Privately, in my mind, I asked her to send me a sign if she was there. Show me something that would make me know that she could see this and feel this beautiful, perfect, day.

Our tour guide said that it was time to get back to the cove so that our boat could return us to our starting point in Hamilton. I got in the kayak and Steve was starting to push us off as he was preparing to get in with me. I reached down to help shove off when suddenly a thumb ring of mine slipped off and fell in the water. Now, the ring fits snugly over my thumb knuckle and I would have to pull and twist it to get it off. It was impossible for it to slide off my thumb.

Sarah had given me the ring for Mother's Day. It was sterling silver and had three words inscribed on it, "Love, Dream, Believe". She had given it to me because of the significance of the word "Believe" and its relevance to Megan's memory. I tried to see where it had fallen, but it seemed to be gone! We were only in a few inches of water and I immediately reached to the spot where it had fallen, but it wasn't there. Steve and I started scooping sand from the bottom, but it was nowhere at all. It was as if it had been swallowed up or somehow disappeared. Our guide came over to ask what was wrong so Steve told him what had happened. He started trying to find it, also. After several minutes I knew that I would not find my ring. I felt so sad to have lost it and thought of the significance it had to both of my daughters and their tie with each other. In the next few moments, I realized something even more profound. This was a sign–a sign that Megan was on the beach with me. She found a way to not only let me know she was there, but she screamed it out to me. There was no way I could miss it or misunderstand it. I told Steve and our guide to stop looking for it. They both looked at me like I was nuts, but I told them that it was alright. The ring would be found someday by someone who needed to read the words on it more than I needed them. It was meant to stay on that beach.

We kayaked away and went back to the boat. As we sailed back toward the main island I saw the little beach in the cove as we passed it. I kept my sunglasses on as I stood there and prayed a private prayer to thank God for this perfect day and a perfect moment of connection. I felt Megan on that beach as clearly as if she had materialized in front of me. I felt Steve as he put his arms around me. He is the only one who saw my tears as we passed. I whispered a goodbye to Megan and knew she was safe.

Mom

My mother was still living in her home, but she was becoming more frail as time went on. In November of 2010, I received a call at 4:30 A.M. from one of her neighbors saying that they thought something was wrong at her house. I went there and found her in her driveway with a flashlight, freezing. She didn't remember why she went out there, but she thought she had been there for a long time. I knew that I couldn't leave her alone at night any longer. From then on, either Sarah or I would stay with her every night. We realized while staying there that she was very confused, more than we could have known. She needed a lot of care.

She digressed more and was beginning to experience falls in her home. By the time another year rolled around I felt that I had no choice, but to admit her to a nursing home. She really needed care twenty-four hours a day by then. I applied on her behalf to the best nursing home in our area and I was fortunate that I was able to admit her there. Now, I knew that she would be safe.

She wasn't very happy initially, in fact, she was quite angry with me for the first three months. After a while, she adjusted to the move and started to make friends. She would go to activities and sing along. She participated in some of the exercise programs, also.

My mother always wanted to be an artist and paint beautiful pictures. She never had a chance to take lessons, which was a big disappointment in her life. She had paints and canvasses, she had instruction books and information on colors, textures, and other miscellaneous things that she used to read to try to paint. What she lacked was an instruction to really get her started.

Once she was in the nursing home we learned that a local artist would go there on occasion and paint with the residents. Imagine my surprise when she started to show me beautiful pictures she had painted. She ended up with a good-sized collection of paintings.

In September of 2012 my sister, Barbara, who was living in Florida, became ill and died within three days of a hospital admission. She had been ill for many years and had often told me that she was ready to go when her time came. I really didn't think she would die that soon. She was only seventy years old, and to me, that still seemed very young. I flew to Florida for the funeral. It was such a sad time, but I knew how she felt and I found comfort in the fact that she felt ready.

I delivered the eulogy at her funeral. I couldn't help but wonder how many more of these I would end up doing. It started to feel like we had too many people on the other side. Now when I thought about it, it seemed like I had more family there than here. We all left the funeral and went to my niece's house. When we got there, we were greeted by a huge double rainbow in the sky. We all felt it was a sign that Barbara was happy where she was.

When I got back home I met with the social worker at the nursing home. They felt that I should tell my mother about Barbara. I wondered how I could do that. My mother had lost two baby boys in the 1940s. Eddy had died in 2004. Now Barbara died. Out of five children she gave birth to, I was the only one still living. How do I find the words to tell her this? How will she react to this? Can she even handle this emotionally? Will she even understand and remember it once I've told her? I worried about what I should do. Finally, I decided that the social worker was probably right. She needed to know; she deserved to know.

I sat down with my mother and made a little small talk. Then I told her that Barbara had gotten sick and had gone to the hospital. I could tell that she knew something important was coming.

I told her what had happened. She just looked at me and said that she knew Barbara hadn't been well for a while. She asked when exactly she had died. So, I told her; I told her that I had flown to Florida and gone to the funeral. I told that I paid respects for all of us. I told all about it, the eulogy included. She asked me why I hadn't told her sooner, by then Barbara had been gone two weeks already. I told her that I didn't want her to get upset, and I was afraid something would happen to her while I was in Florida so I waited until I got back to share the news with her. She looked at me and said, "Susan, I know why you didn't tell me before now. You just didn't have the heart to say it to me." She was right about that. The same way that my mother was always right. She was right and proper and dignified her entire life. In that moment I aspired to be like her as much as I ever had. At ninety-three years old she still was the most compassionate and loving woman I have ever known.

At Christmas, I brought my laptop to the nursing home. We booted it up and prepared to Skype with the rest of the family. Mom loved seeing everyone. She couldn't believe how amazing it was to talk with them through the computer. She was really happy, but then I saw a change in her. She looked at me and asked, "Where is Barbara? Tell her to come over so I can see her, too." I didn't know what to say. She realized when I didn't say anything. Her face just said it all. She told me she was tired and asked if we could stop now. My dear mother had forgotten that her daughter had died. But in that moment, she knew the truth. Barbara was not there for Christmas. I understood how my mother felt to realize that her child was absent on the holiday.

Inscription for A Gravestone

In May of 2013, we traveled to Florida to attend my niece's wedding. The wedding was taking place in a beautiful park in Vero Beach with three gazebos that were all connected. She had brought my niece, Darleen, and me to see it when we were there for Barbara's funeral. During the wedding planning, the family started talking about all of the family members who have died in recent years. For each person who had died, there were some family members who could not attend due to work or other restraints. These things are difficult when family members live so far apart. Most of the family was going to be present at the wedding, though.

My nieces were also concerned that they had not had an opportunity yet to tend to my sister, Barbara's, ashes. We decided this would be a good time to do that. As our discussions evolved we came to the decision that this was a great opportunity to hold a private memorial for everyone that had passed. Discussions regarding the logistics of where and when to hold the memorial pursued. My sister wanted her ashes in the sea, but determining an appropriate beach was difficult due to laws pertaining to the disposal of remains.

We decided that a good place would be the same park as the wedding, but in an area, that was on a riverside that would carry her ashes to the sea. They chose the perfect spot for us to gather. On the morning after the wedding, we all gathered there. We had an opportunity to each speak about our feelings and contribute to memories about my sister's second husband, my father, Eddy, Megan, Joshua, and of course Barbara.

I read the poem *Inscription For A Gravestone* by Robinson Jeffers at the memorial service. The poem holds the meaning of what I believe it must be like to cross to the other side. The following lines from it hold a special meaning to me:

> I admired the beauty while I was human, now I am part
> of the beauty.
>
> I wander in the air,
> Being mostly gas and water, and flow in the ocean;
> I touch you and Asia at the same moment.

It describes the ability to wander the Earth, to be a part of it. I believe that when we die we are still here, but in another reality, another realm of being, but still present in the lives of the people we love. We can be anywhere and everywhere. We let go of the pain, the trials that are living as we know it. We celebrate the joy and beauty of our being on a level that as humans we can never truly know. Our reality becomes more beautiful and free than we could ever imagine in our human shells. The spirit soars.

I believe that my whole family felt a close bond and love for each other to finally celebrate the life of all of these people whom we loved and had lost. I think the memorial held even more meaning because we could acknowledge the grief we all felt, and we were able to validate and comfort each other. The love that we have as a family was felt deeply and fully in that clearing by the river.

Please Touch Me

Some things just don't seem possible when we think in practical ways. Other things are so spiritual that it is difficult, if not impossible, to describe them in practical terms. Some skeptics will never allow themselves to open their hearts and minds enough to accept what can't be seen. I know there are people who will not be able to accept or believe the next few paragraphs. I only know how it was for me.

In 2013 I was attending Eastern Connecticut State University. I finally had the opportunity to finish my Bachelor's Degree. It was a long time coming and a dream come true for me. My biggest bucket list item! One of the toughest challenges for me was that every day, as I drove to the school, I passed the place on the road where Megan's accident had taken place. At first, it was almost impossible for me to drive past, and several times I stopped and got out my car just to be there, in that spot. I managed to transform the area on the side of the road from a place of unspeakable sadness to a place of bittersweet remembrance for myself.

For some unknown reason, this spot had been chosen out of the entire universe to be the spot my baby would die. That moment in time, and how I imagine it to have been for her, came together right there. I would remember the words she had once told the psychic–"It was a beautiful place to die".

Eventually, I became accustomed to driving past it twice a day, five days a week. I would make the sign of the cross every time. I would say something, either "I love you, Megan", or "God bless you Megan", or some other pertinent little phrase aimed at her and God.

One day in August, as I started down the road that silly song that she loved came on the radio. As "*Save a Horse, Ride a Cowboy*" played I thought of Megan and her funny ways. I said out loud in my car, "Hi,

Megan, I know you're here with me!" As that song ended, the next song that came on is one that I can't hear without feeling the sadness of my loss. The song is "*If I Die Young*". Now I knew she was with me for sure. I started talking to her and crying. As I started to cry harder I realized that I was right in front of the spot where she died. I said to her that I know she is around me a lot of the time, but it isn't enough. I told her that I needed her to find a way to touch me; to physically touch me. I told her that I was ready and I wouldn't be scared. I promised her that it wouldn't upset me, that it would comfort me. I needed it.

By the time I got on the college campus I had composed myself and prepared myself to go to my four-hour summer class.

During the class, the instructor was talking about various services in the local community. He told us to look up different places and research the work that is done there. It was part of an assignment that would be due the next day.

That night I sat in my room on my laptop searching for information about some of the places the instructor had spoken about. As I did this I went to Google Earth to see where they were located in relation to the campus. I moved around on Google Earth and looked at other things surrounding the area. I ended up looking at the accident scene from Google Earth. It looked very different from this view.

I noticed something in the lower portion of the screen. It looked like a clearing with a circle in the middle. I remembered the psychic telling me that there was a place just past where she had died where there was something in the middle. Gary had said, "There is a monument or some type of marker not far from there. The marker is not for her. It's been there a long time. If I look for it, it's almost on a hill. I can see the landmark near there. You'll know the spot. You'll find her there." As I zoomed in closer I realized that what I was looking at was a cemetery that I passed every day, but had never gone into. I never realized that there was a circular roadway in the middle with a tree planted in the middle of the circle. I thought that must be what she was referring to.

I went to bed around ten o'clock that night and fell into a deep sleep, as I was exhausted. I became partially awake in the middle of the night but did not reach a complete awake state. As I lay there I felt light and

I saw myself lying in the exact position I was in, but under that tree in the middle of the cemetery. I wasn't sure how I got there but knew I was safe. From the distance, I saw Megan coming toward me. As she got closer I was aware that she was communicating something to me, but she wasn't speaking aloud. I just knew she was relaying a message to me. She was telling me that she was going to touch me, but that I shouldn't be afraid. I told her that I was ready and would not be scared.

Suddenly I felt a tingling, like an electric current, come into my feet and travel up my body until my entire body felt the current within me. Then it traveled back down my body and out of my feet. I saw her smile and then she left. I fell back into a deep sleep.

When I awoke the next morning, I was overwhelmed with the feeling of joy and wanted to celebrate what had happened. The only problem was that I thought anyone I told would think I had really lost it and that I was crazy.

Steve believed me when I told him, and so did Sarah. I didn't tell anyone else for a very long time.

Mom, Part 2

The following September my mother was hospitalized with a myocardial infarction. The emergency room doctors asked me to sign a surgical release for her. I told them I would talk with her. I looked at her and explained what was happening. She said, "No. No surgery. Remember what you promised me." I told her that she would not have surgery. I was keeping my promise. She improved enough to go back to the nursing home.

We had a small birthday party for her when she turned ninety-four. Sarah and Alex were there. Darleen came down from New Hampshire. Rosy and his wife, Anne, who I had developed a relationship with and felt she was like another sister-in-law were there. Of course, Steve and I hosted it. We had takeout food, birthday cake, and ice cream. We all knew this would be her last birthday. When Rosy left he told her how much he loved her and then left, trying to hide tears that we all knew couldn't be hidden.

The holidays came and I sat in her room talking about what she would like to give everyone for Christmas this year. She didn't know what to do. That's when I got an idea. I took out all of her paintings. I started asking her if she wanted to give certain ones to different members of the family. We picked out and assigned appropriate paintings to each member of the family including Alex and one for Rebecca's son, Landon, her great-great-grandchild. I packaged all of the paintings and shipped them out to everyone in Florida. I shipped other ones to my nephew in Las Vegas, also.

On Christmas we went to see her; Steve and I, Sarah and Alex, and Darleen. We had a delicious dinner in the dining room. After dinner, I set up my laptop and we Skyped with the family. She watched as each one opened their painting from her. The "oohs" and "ahhs" were breathtaking. She was smiling so wide and so proud. She kept looking at me and saying, "I painted that!" It was the best Christmas! Mom held on a little while longer, but after New Year's Day, we knew that her time was coming. I think she had held on for the holidays. She was tired and she was slowly letting go.

I started a new job on January 14th that year. I had only worked two days when I was called at work and told that I should go to see my mom if I wanted to be with her. I left work and went straight to her. She was wide awake, but she was not talking. I held her hand and spoke with her. After a little while, Sarah came in and then Darleen arrived. We all stayed with her. She held our hands and didn't want to let go. There were two of us holding each of her hands all day. I couldn't get over how bony her hands felt. She had lost so much weight that her hands felt like skeleton hands with just a thin layer of skin on them. We took turns sitting with her, but none of us left her side. She refused to fall asleep. At one point I noticed that she had slid down in her bed and looked uncomfortable. I asked two nurses if they could please lift her up so she would be better supported. As they lifted her, she looked up at the top corner of the room and said, "My son!" I looked at her and asked, "Do you see Eddy?" She nodded and said, "Yes!" A little while after that she tried to say something else, but I couldn't understand it. Sarah thought that she had said, "I'm dying." She never said another word.

Sarah and Darleen left in the evening. Sarah had to take care of Alex and Darleen went with her to stay at my house for the night. I asked for a roll-away cart to sleep on. About eleven o'clock she was asleep and I was exhausted so I laid down to rest. I was woken by the nurse around two o'clock. She had come in to check on Mom. She was awake so the nurse asked if she wanted her pain medication. She nodded. The nurse went down the hall to get it. She was back in the room within five minutes. When she came in my mother had crossed. That's when she woke me. At first, I felt terrible that I had slept through it. The nurse explained to me that she knew I was there; she knew she would be found quickly; she chose her moment, just as my father had chosen his moment.

I was left alone in her room to say my goodbye. I held her hand and spoke to her, once again telling her how much I loved her. Then I climbed onto her bed with her. I held her in my arms and told her I was there for her. I held her until the cold traveled through her body and I felt her spirit had risen.

We had to tell my grandson, Alex, that his great-grandmother had died. I tried to explain it to him as simply as I could. He had been studying about Martin Luther King Day in school, as it was the end of January. He looked at me and asked, "Is she dead like Martin Luther King?" I told him, "Yes, just like Martin Luther King, she will never come back." He was able to understand and accept her death in this way. It made me think about when I was a child. I understood death more after I experienced John F. Kennedy's death. Children need a way of relating to it on their own terms.

My house became very cold. For days we couldn't seem to make it warmer. We turned up the heat and we lit fires in the wood stove. Nothing took the chill out.

During the next night, I was in an in-between state of sleep and wake. I felt like it was around three in the morning, but I wasn't sure. I was aware that Steve was in bed beside me and it was freezing cold. Then I became aware that I felt my mother's hand holding my hand, thin and skeletal with just a thin layer of skin, like the day before. I held it and caressed it. It felt as real as it possibly could. Then it slipped away, out of my grasp.

I fell back to sleep and slept soundly after that. When I woke around seven in the morning Steve was still lying next to me. I turned to him and told him what I had experienced. He said that at that same time he had woken and felt the room was freezing. He had become aware of the smell of cookies baking and had wondered who was baking at that time. He knew Darleen was sleeping on our couch and it wouldn't be her. It certainly wouldn't be Sarah, either. We knew then that it was Megan. She had helped my mother to come to me and let me know that she was alright. She was safe on the Other Side and with her loved ones.

I have two photos of my father on the wall of my dining room. One is of him as a young man in his Army uniform; the other is one of him at around seventy years old. Above them is a shadow box with his service medals, dog tags, and an American flag.

I also have a framed photo in the hallway of my mother-in-law. There is a copy of a letter that was sent to the local newspaper after she died with a tribute to the person she was. I have often wished I could have known her, but she died before I met my husband. When we came home in the evening after my mother's wake the framed photo of my mother-in-law was on the floor. The frame was broken, but not the glass. We couldn't figure how or why it had fallen. It had been securely there for years without ever moving. Finally, we concluded that she was trying to let us know that she was there and offering her love and support to us.

After the funeral my house became warm once again.

Another Home Visit

On June 8, 2014, I held another group meeting with Gary McKinstry at my home. In attendance were my husband, Steve, Sarah, and my niece, Darleen, and a friend of ours, Karen. We all sat around in my living room and the meeting started.

An older female came through. "This is me and this is how it was supposed to be. She said that she could be kind of a pain." He asked if we knew who was coming through. I said that it could be one of two people. I was thinking that it was either my sister, Barbara or my mother. Gary said it was the smaller one. We knew that had to be my mother because my sister was large and my mother was very petite.

Gary went on, "She was very nice, but everything had to be in its place. It's not perfect, but it's her place. 'This is my stuff'. She's not mean. It's like you were her support system somehow. She said that you came in and did things; you fixed things. There's a 'thank you' part, but there is also an 'I'm sorry' part. No offense, but this lady wasn't always understanding all of the time. 'I wish I could have been more understanding when I was here. It's not like I gave you a hard time, but I did give you a hard time.' She felt like sometimes even simple things were harder, she didn't mean to be like that. As much as she would have liked to change, she couldn't change."

"She's in a dress like she's going somewhere. Usually, she would wear slacks, but this time she's dressed up. It's like, 'I'm going someplace important, you know.' She's sorry that you were the one that had to take care of things. There was someone else that was supposed to help, but they didn't do much. This is like 'They should have, they could have', she understood it. She's sorry that you got left holding the bag. I'm sorry about that part, too. I don't know why the chest is bothering her like

I can breathe, but not well. It's like they put her on morphine to slow things down, but not enough to knock her out." My mother finally died due to congestive heart failure. She was on morphine at the very end to ease the pain and relax her, but she remained alert right up to the end.

"She's in her kitchen right now. She's there because she wants to be there. In the other room, the TV is on and the sound is low, but I can hear it. Wheel of Fortune is on. I think she had a thing for Pat Sajack. 'My show is on.' She has a package of Fig Newtons, she has a cup of tea, and she is waiting for the phone to ring. It'll be someone checking up on her. By the way, she won't give me a cookie. I said that I like Fig Newtons, too. She just has one sleeve of Fig Newtons, like she's rationing them. She said that she's having three of them." He told her that she could have four, but she said no, "only three." My mother would sit at her kitchen table and eat three Fig Newtons or graham crackers with her decaf coffee while she waited for the Wheel of Fortune to come on each night. She never ate more than what she considered one serving.

"She is using the same cup and said it's the same cup every night. She said this is the one I use. Everything had to be the same. She's in her housecoat. Not a bathrobe, she said it's a housecoat. 'I have a lot of work to do.' You know what's funny, I don't ever see your father with her. She must have gone on for quite a while without him. They would be together, but they come across as being apart for a long time". (My mother lived more than fourteen years after my father passed.)

She said that we had done a good job, "I know you were busy, but don't worry about it. You had a lot going on, so don't worry. OK? I mean this for real." Gary went on, "She had her family and that was the most important thing to her. I don't know who Roger is, but she said that it was a shame about Roger. Her program is coming on now. She said that she doesn't care much for Jeopardy. She said that the questions are fixed, anyway. There's no way to fix the Wheel of Fortune, but no normal person knows the answers to the Jeopardy questions. On Wheel of Fortune, the people make sense. She's watching the weather like it's a big deal." My mother lived by weather reports. Gary said that she was watching Bruce Schwoegler. This was really amazing because she always watched that particular weatherman that was on a Boston news station.

One time when I was young he was in town to be in a local parade and she had to go just because she was so thrilled to see him. There is actually a picture of him in one of her photo albums.

"She was hurt three times. Once is bad enough, twice is horrendous, but in a lifetime, you should never be hurt three times." I said that she lost three sons and a daughter. The daughter was recent. He said, "She didn't get the daughter part, which is good. Losing the sons was bad enough; the daughter would have killed her. At least one of the sons was really young and that was really bad. The others had a chance to live a little."

"Her mind was a little confused before her passing. It feels like she was a little confused. 'The time sequences were off, and if I didn't understand everything going on around me, I'm sorry. Suddenly I would relive things and go back and forth. Some moments I would feel really with it, and then some moments I would be really gone.' She didn't like that, and felt like 'why can't I remember?' She was black and white–there was no gray with this lady."

"By the way, you did please her. Understand that. She knows you worried that you didn't do enough, but you did. It's the reverse; she knows that she didn't give you enough credit, OK? In her mind, you did everything that you were supposed to do. OK?"

"Do you know what a brooch is? Someplace there is one connected to her. It's important. It's not worth a lot of money, but it is valuable. Find it. She's telling you to wear it." I knew exactly what he was referring to.

She looked at Steve and said that she wouldn't pick on him. Gary said, "She respected you. It's almost like you're the guy who fixes things. You always come in and fix everything. 'By the way, I only had to ask once. If something needed to be fixed you would always get to it' That's how she felt. She had a lot of respect for you. She only had to ask once."

"Who's the cancer lady? She's very tiny like she had lost a lot of weight before she died. She's been gone a little while. She didn't want to be seen or be remembered like that. She went downhill very fast." I thought of one of my mother's sisters who had died in April. We were told by the family that we could not see her. "She fell hard and couldn't do anything. The family was following her wishes."

He looked at Darleen, "there is a young energy associated with you. It feels traumatic. They weren't supposed to go; it left a lot of people upset. It feels really confused–like the world stopped. By the way, it's not just one, but two. Almost like tragedy is bad, but this is really bad. The family felt like celebrations are coming and what do we do? They are saying, 'Tell them to have fun.' Actually, there are three that have passed. Two feel tragic, but the third feels almost natural. It didn't happen together, but they are together there."

"Somebody had a heart issue and died suddenly. By the time he got to the hospital he had died. He had a dry sense of humor. He'd be thinking this was very funny. He could do things naturally. He didn't need a book to tell him how to do things. It feels like there should have been a box of tools around him." We thought this was a reference to Steve's father. By the time he was found he was already gone. He was a carpenter, so this accounted for the knowledge of doing things and the toolbox.

"Who's Ernie? Not Ernest, Ernie. For some reason, Ernie is showing me the outside, like I want to be outside. I feel comfortable in the woods and it feels good. If he saw your backyard with all of the trees he would say 'this feels like heaven'. He's a nice man, never hurt anybody. He's just coming through to say 'Hi". He hasn't talked to anyone for a while. He's really, really happy. He's sitting on a log right now. He remembers you as a kid. To him, you are a kid. 'Say hi to the kid.'" My grandpa was named Ernest, my cousin was named after him and was called Ernie, but I never heard him called Ernest. He was into hunting and fishing and breeding dogs. Ernie was about fifteen years older than me and felt like a was a kid to him.

"I know who is coming home. I am blocking someone out right now. Do you understand what I mean? If I don't, she will take over the whole reading. I was afraid of that today. I had to tell her to hold off because I have to tell other people things." Megan kept trying to come through, but Gary tried to hold her off for a while so that others could come through. He was concerned that she would monopolize the reading.

"There is a male coming through who feels that he has to come home. This is traumatic." We thought this was connected to Darleen, and we believed it was Joshua at first. "I need to ask you a question. I see a group of people in a hospital room. Like a vigil. Like we have to decide if we should shut it down?" Darleen started to think it was her mother, but we soon realized that it wasn't.

Karen said that she thought it was for her. Her significant other had died recently and they had to make a decision. He said that it was a group decision being made to detach and unplug or not. "I need to tell you not to ever feel guilty. I know you probably don't, but it was a good decision. Everybody knew what to do, but no one knew what to do. Everyone was standing there wondering. 'Make sure you tell her it was the right decision, OK?' It's kind of laid back, it feels like he's OK and what's the big deal? I don't know who shouldn't be alone, but you shouldn't be. He needs to tell you that. He wants to thank you. By the way, it wasn't a bad life. It was good. Somebody is at the nineteenth hole. Like having adult beverages–it's cocktail hour. I don't know why his stomach was hurting. I don't know how he screwed up, but he's saying that he did. He's sorry. I feel like a little boy that did something naughty. 'Everything was good, but I screwed up.' By the way, if the tables were turned he couldn't handle it. It's almost like if things were different he wasn't as strong as you are. Weird question–did you buy him a shirt? It may still be somewhere." Karen said, "Yes, his nephew wore it to his funeral." "By the way, he is not upset that his nephew wore it. Everything was messed up around him. There is a fun part of him. He was the kind of guy that when he was in the room you want to laugh and have fun. I don't know what you have to do, but it's OK to do whatever you need to do. I'm sure you have made decisions since he passed, but make the decisions you need. Trust yourself. After he passed he knows you were yelling at him. He says, that the message was received."

"This is really weird. What is the self-induced death due to bad decisions? It was not on purpose. There was no coming back from something. 'I shouldn't have been gone, but I'm gone.' It sounds like they wasted their life. 'There were moments when I felt OK, but then I slipped again. I screwed up.' The passing didn't hurt. She wanted to withdraw and be alone. She pulled back from people a lot. She could have been helped, but she would have had to accept it. It's nobody's fault. You can't force somebody to do something. Thank you, you didn't condemn me. That's the thank you. I'm not in pain anymore." I believe this was my sister, Barbara. She made some bad lifestyle choices and had poor health as a result. In the last few years of her life, she kept telling me that she knew she couldn't go back and change her health. She felt that she had "screwed up" her life and it was too late to change.

Gary asked, "Where's the lake back there? I was driving here and was told (by a spirit) that there is a lake back there. You can't see it well from the road. There's a man worrying." There is a pond in the back area behind the house that you can't see from the road, but we didn't have any idea who was telling Gary this.

"There are two factors coming through. One is that a bad decision was made, and the other is an accident, confusion, things happened fast, all at the same time. Everything was close, you didn't get a break. One thing happened and then another thing happened. There is like a loop up there and it all happened at the same time.

There's a long road I'm on and I'm tired. I'm going someplace, but it is taking a long time. I don't know what this is about. We're traveling somewhere–it's a trip. It's a good memory." Darleen and I both started thinking that this was representing a trip that Rosy, Darleen and my mother went on around 2002. Rosy drove them to Florida to visit with everyone down there just before Christmas. They celebrated an early Christmas together while they were there. "Thank you for the memory."

"An older gentleman is coming through. He's saying he doesn't need the damn walker. He could get around without it." We figured this was Darleen's father-in-law coming through. "He came across gruff."

There's a girl that says, "You have to let me go". He said that this was not Megan. It's not about keeping her. In order to get past things, you have to face them and accept them before you can move through them.

"Somebody has a dirt bike. Not a Harley." We never figured out who this was.

"I've got the girl." (Megan) "She's going up the road and then coming back. She could take up the whole day with messages. Most of the people I have read go away, but she is still here. On my way here I felt her in the car, and I was like, 'Is this a command performance? Am I going to be just bringing her through?' She's bouncy. It's good energy. She's still here. When I took a break, and was on the front porch, I spoke with her. She wants to know 'How old is the child now?'" Alex was six at the time. "She's checking in on the kid. She always keeps an eye on him."

"Where's the house with the walk-in basement? It's like I am going in the basement and I don't use the front door or the back door. I don't know why. Hey, I'm back! It feels normal." We explained that this house has a walk-in basement, and we always use the basement door instead of other doors. "In her case time has stood still in a good way. The energy part feels good. The memory of coming home feels good to her. It feels like I'm getting ready to go out, very social and fun. It's kind of funny that every time I see her it's never gray. The sun is always shining around her."

"There's a friend with her on the other side. Someone named Ann, someone she knew, a young lady. By the way, she's dressed in slacks and a blouse. Not informal, but not formal. The slacks are not quite black, but they are dark. This is not what she wore the day she died." I think Gary was describing the grey slacks and pink satin blouse we dressed her in to be laid out. It was kind of her way of acknowledging the outfit.

"I keep seeing a Volkswagen Beetle." Sarah acknowledged that Megan had a Volkswagen Jetta for a while. She's showing a shiny black Volkswagen Beetle. I said that my brother had one. This is her way of saying she has been with him. She's with her grandmother." (My mother.)

"By the way, how's the engineer doing?" He looked at Steve and said, "By the way, in case you wonder how this works, it's a vibration of harmonics. The reason memories are not trapped but out in the stratosphere is that on a particle level what happens is that everything stays in pieces because of vibrational harmonics. Your structure is held together because you vibrate at a very high rate, that's how you are actually, physically held together. In fact, the whole universe has a vibrational pattern. If the pattern stops then you dissipate and break apart. So when a person passes, the vibrational part, the energetic part, changes, fades and falls apart. The physical body doesn't fall apart, but the vibrational energy pattern tends to dissipate, it just changes form and goes into a different dimension. There are multiple universes operating simultaneously, and for whatever reason, in order to connect to somebody, you change your pattern. All you're doing is slowing down your vibrational rate and you're jumping from one pattern to the next. That's why it's not a perfect connection because if you did have a perfect connection then you wouldn't be here any longer."

"If you notice what I'm doing, I'm pretty relaxed. Like I'm having fun. If I don't relax and have fun with it my pattern is too high, and my energy level would be too high. In meditation you practice relaxation to change your vibrational pattern to change location, you don't physically change location, but part of the essence of meditation is to go from one place to another. When I say that she is here, she's not physically here, but she comes through theoretically because she's on the same wavelength or frequency."

"She probably has good vibes around you guys, your energy pattern is in sync. Some people, no matter how hard they try, will never get through because the energy is not there, but in your case, you are basically within that balance. So, she has the opportunity to come through. By the way, it doesn't mean that if you move from this house that you will never see her again. It doesn't work that way. She connects with people, not the place. It means that it's not just this house, it's that she connects with you and will be with you even if you leave here."

"One way to help change the vibrational pattern is to count from ten to one, visualize opening a doorway and going through it. After a while you don't need to do that, you just do it." This reminded me of the time when Gary told me to visualize Megan on a beach walking toward me. The closer she would walk to me the closer our connection would become. It also made me think of the time when she met me in the cemetery in my semi-sleeping state.

"The young lady that came through a little while ago wasn't quite done. I have to finish this part off. She wouldn't be mad at you, but she feels irritated at someone. It's because somebody won't accept her passing. You feel sad, but you accept closure eventually. Your daughter is always rushing around. She still doesn't have time. When she was here she had so much going on that she never had time. This is a very tranquil afternoon, but in her case, it's as if she is blowing in and then leaving. 'But I'll be back. I'll always be back.' For now, I have to go, not far, I just have to go."

That's the way Megan was. She had so much to do that she never had the time to do it all. She was always in a rush to fit it all in. "'I wish I could stay, but I can't.' It's a good feeling. She didn't waste her time, she packed everything in. 'I packed every ounce in that I could.' It's a good feeling. 'I didn't miss much.' She's not alone; she's got a group of girls. She's wearing a dark maroon gown. 'I had a really good life.' It feels like you're the one she really didn't get the chance to talk with. It wasn't on purpose, it was just an accident. No one messed up or anything, it just happened. No guilt. There is still love."

Gary told us that he had a son who had passed. People asked him how you get through that. His response is that you don't. The second part of it is that there is no guilt because nothing was wrong. I said that "I don't feel guilty and I don't feel anger I just miss her. I've come a long way." Gary said that he can see that I have come a long way.

He said that Alex can see her. "She is playful energy. Pretty soon he won't see her anymore. He'll get too busy and little kids see people when they are not busy, then they start to grow up and they get too busy to see people. The spirit sort of fades. When they are older they can pick them up again. He might ask you at some point who the lady is. But if he doesn't see her for a while, don't panic. It doesn't mean that she's not around."

He looked at Darleen, "I'm sorry I only had one major connection to you. The only unfinished one, you have a mixture of people. Two younger energies, they were very traumatic. I felt like they wanted forgiveness, but one didn't. I am getting more auditory signs right now. I feel like there is a whole group of people on the other side. They are holding back on communication. There is fun energy. He's kind of like a hippy. This was a cool, laid-back guy." I thought it was Eddy, but Gary said that it wasn't Eddy. Darleen seemed to think it was someone she knew that the rest of us didn't know.

He said that she was from a family with eight siblings. I said that my mother was one of eight sisters. "One by one we all passed," Gary said there were two left. I said that there were three left. He said, "No two. One is going soon. They are making room for one. There will be two left soon. Get prepared. Then the last two will last for a while. They were nice, it was a good family." One of my aunts died within four months of this reading, leaving two of the siblings.

I said that I had something I wanted to tell him about and get his opinion on it. I began telling him the story of the time during the prior summer when I was driving to school and asked Megan to touch me. I went on to tell about being in the semi-awake state in the night and seeing her in the cemetery. I described the feeling of a tingling sensation, almost electric, that started in my feet and traveled up and through me as I lay in bed. Until this point, the only people who knew about this were Steve and Sarah.

He said that when he feels this type of connection with someone it feels almost like a low voltage electrical charge creeping up his body. It starts at the toes and literally rises to the head and then back. "What you're talking about literally is almost like you can feel like a flush of energy and then it comes down. I use the term "contact" to describe it. When you get the chills, and feel someone is there it's the beginning. How far does it go? There's a point of a pretty solid connection sometimes. So, yeah, what happened to you–was it some sort of contact? It's not the same as what happens in a reading, but that communication is sensed."

When someone is talking to him, he understands the words, but he's not really hearing the words. It's almost like he gets their thought pattern. "It's almost like telepathy–you don't hear them speak, but you hear their message." He said that what happened to me was on that same line. "Usually about two-thirty or three o'clock in the morning is the time when you would get the most. The reason is that it's a very open time. The world is quiet and their energy levels come up, and our energy levels is at a static. If you are in a dream state at that point you are going through the REM state, and you're open to whatever is coming through, and it will really hit you. So, you're not crazy. At that point everything sets you up for that, all of the circumstances were perfect and it just kind of led you into it. You just went into it really easily. Was it real? It's as real as it is. I don't know how to explain that. People might think you were dreaming." I explained that I was hesitant to tell people about it because I feared they would think I had really lost my mind. Or else they would think that I just really have to deal with my daughter dying. Gary said that I really need to let it go, and accept that she is here. "This work is something that you can't fake. If someone wants to be here they will come through. If they wanted to die, even if it wasn't suicide, they will not be here. They are in their own place, and have found their freedom."

Darleen asked if Gary sometimes draws from the hopes of people that are present, and not just from those who have passed. He said that he loves this question. "I thought for a while that that would happen. Like maybe I'm catching what they want to hear. I really thought that until I ran into some stuff that people didn't know. I had two sisters who came to see me. I started talking about their father who loved to dress in a special outfit and wear certain shoes. He and their mother would go out dancing. The sisters told me that I was bad at this. They said that their father never danced, didn't like to dance, and the mother was fat. They said that everything I said was wrong. They left. A few weeks later they called and said that they were very sorry. They had found out that before they were born their parents used to go out dancing all of the time, in fact, their father had special shoes." They weren't open to his reading because it wasn't what they knew, but it was what Gary had seen. A lot of the time things he sees in a reading are things that he doesn't understand the meaning of. Later, it might fit.

He gave Megan as another example. At this point, he felt like he knew her, and wondered when he came to the house if he was expecting her so he made her come through. But, no, she comes through with something different each time I see him and he sees Megan.

I told Gary that an example of this happened to me when I saw him that very first time and he told me about the "break in my family tree". I had no idea what that meant until my father's interment and my uncle told me about my great grandmother being an unwed mother in the late eighteen hundredths. Gary was surprised to hear that and said that he would never have known that at the time. In other words, he doesn't always understand the message that he gets, but he conveys it the best that he can and hopes it makes sense to the person hearing it.

If you were on the other side and you had a second to come through– what would you want your message to be? And how would you convey it so that others would understand and realize who you were? Think about that.

Gary said that sometimes someone comes through that is not related to the people present. For example, when he is at my house someone going by might come through and not make any sense to any of us. At this reading when the guy on the dirt bike came through for a moment is a perfect example.

I mentioned the spirits in the house. He said that he didn't sense them today. I admitted that I had smudged the house before he came to cleanse it of miscellaneous spirits. He said that they are annoying, but not evil. We have learned that we have to be firm with the spirits.

Steve told the story of spirits in the house that he lived in in Westerly, Rhode Island. The house had been built in the seventeen hundredths. That house was actually haunted. He got up once during the night to go to the bathroom. He walked out to the hall, which was moonlit. He saw a shadow down the hall and then describes two "whoosh-whoosh" feelings. He was suddenly aware of a feeling that they had gone right through him. There was also a time when something held him down on the bed. He felt an enormous pressure on him and he couldn't get up for a few minutes. Then it was gone but it was very cold.

Gary said that the reason the temperature drops when a spirit comes through is because of energy inversion. They need to pull energy to manifest, which changes the dynamics in the room. He described a reading in a home where everyone in the room felt cold and was pulling throw blankets on. One of the ladies' husbands came in and commented on how cold it was in the room. He checked the heat and said that the thermostat was fine and the rest of the house was warm. That was the only room that was cold. After Gary left it was warm in there once again. Steve and I told him about the time after my mother died when she and Megan came through together. Steve woke to the smell of cookies and was very cold. He turned the heat up because it was so cold.

People on the other side can't stop things from happening, but they can "nudge". Steve told the story of finding the dragonfly pendant in the Umbrella Factory. In his version of the story, he handed the pendant to the saleslady and asked her not to talk with him because he was sneaking it out to give to me on Mother's Day. He describes it "jumping out of his pocket" in the parking lot and realizing that he had to give it to me right then. He felt the "nudge" that Gary was talking about. He said that it was literally on fire in his pocket.

Gary said that there are also evil places on the other side of the spectrum that he won't go near. There are bad things that he sees that he can't or won't talk about.

Megan Sends a Sign

I was alone at home one day and in the dining room going over bills and paperwork. I heard a noise in the living room. I walked in to investigate what could have caused the noise. I noticed on the top of a cabinet that two pictures had fallen over spontaneously. The one in the back was a photo of Megan holding Snuggles on Christmas morning, 2006–her last Christmas. It had fallen forward and knocked over a black and white photo from my childhood. Megan had worked with my mom that Christmas to pick out four photos from my childhood and get copies made and framed for my mom to give to me. I picked up both photos and put them back the way they belonged. I said out loud, "Hi, Megan. Thanks for the sign."

I spoke with my niece, Darleen, over the phone a little later that day. She told me that earlier in the day she was going through some things and came across the picture of Megan on Christmas, holding Snuggles and photos of me opening my gift from my mom. She asked if I remembered the photos Megan had gotten framed for her to give to me. I was so surprised that Darleen was looking at those same photos. I told her about those same two pictures falling over earlier that day. It seems that these two things were happening within moments of each other.

Darleen started talking more about that Christmas. She also had a photo of Megan opening the gift she had given her. It was a jewelry box with a thumb ring in it. The photo shows Megan holding the box with the ring on and giving a "thumbs up". The following text messages between Darleen and me transpired later:

Darleen: A sign today! I came home with groceries. I have a wine cart that had two fancy napkin rings on it... Walked in and one of the napkin rings is way in the middle of the floor! Who do you think it was?

Me: I don't know. That's an odd one! Wow, have to figure that out.

Darleen: I was pondering it, we were talking about the thumb ring I got Megan. Could it be Megan? Could that be the sign for a ring?

Me: A symbol of a ring makes sense. Maybe it was Megan.

Darleen: As I think about it more, the link makes more sense.

Me: If Megan caused the pictures to fall over at my house to let me know that she was here, and then led you to the same pictures at your house to let you know she was with you, maybe she realized we were talking about it and comparing our experiences. If she knew we talked about the ring and the other picture, could she have moved the napkin ring as a symbol of a ring? It's not really that farfetched. She's around all the time, and this is just full-circle communication. I love it. It tells me she knew we discussed the photos falling, me looking at the photos and the photo of her with the ring.

Darleen: These events are amazingly connected. The napkin ring was too far away from the wine cart to have fallen there. I tried nudging it off the cart to see where it would fall, and it kept falling right next to it, not where I found it. And when I got home with groceries, I had my arms full and had to stop and say, what's that? It was cool.

Me: She sent an amazing sign to us. Also, I believe that she had both photos fall over to let me know that she is with my mother. I think that was the original message.

Darleen: I agree. The photo of you hugging Grandma shows that as well. Such an incredible story. I just love it. And I love that we witnessed it together.

We are all connected in spirit. These are the things that keep me going on through my grief. The fact is that loved ones that have passed are always present. It brings such comfort and joy to me that I know I will be with them again. If I look back at the poem I read at our little family memorial I feel that it just may be true that the spirits can be in more than one place at a time. (I touch you and Asia at the same moment)

A Family Gathering

In September of 2014, I made plans to inter my mother's ashes. Her ashes were to go in the same plot as my father and my brother's ashes were in. I made the arrangements through the funeral home to have the gravesite opened. I contacted the immediate family, including everyone in Florida and my nephew in Las Vegas. I was surprised when several of the Florida family decided to make the trip.

There would be five guests from Florida staying at my house. Darleen was coming down from New Hampshire, and Alex wanted to stay over because Landon would be there. Although Alex was seven years old and Landon was five years old, they had never met.

I worked hard to figure out sleeping arrangements for all of these guests. We had a place for everyone to sleep along with bedding and pillows for everyone. The guests arrived on Friday night and we enjoyed having dinner and catching up on all of the family news.

On Saturday Sarah arrived at the house with her fiancé and we all went to the cemetery to inter the ashes. I had asked the funeral director if we could take a little of my father's ashes out of his urn so that I could have them. I also wanted a little of my mother's ashes to keep for myself. There was an extra cost to this, but it meant a lot to me, so I followed through with my request. My niece had asked if a little of my sister's ashes could be buried with my mother. I knew that this was a very unusual request and I wasn't sure if it would be allowed.

We took turns saying a few words about my mother. Even Alex spoke about his great-grandmother and what she meant to him. He said that he was glad that he knew her. I prayed that he would never forget her because she loved him so much.

The funeral director said that we should leave while they put the urn in the ground and covered it. I remembered being told the same thing when we interred my father's ashes. This time I didn't want to do it that way. I had taken care of my mother in so many ways through the past years that I truly wanted to do this last thing for her. I placed the urn in the burial plot myself. I cried and shook as I did this, but I knew it just felt right. I asked my niece if she had brought some of my sister's ashes and she said that she had them with her. I asked if the funeral director would look the other way and they walked a few feet away and turned their back to me. I sprinkled my sister's ashes on my mother's urn and covered it with dirt. We all put some dirt in, said a prayer, and walked away.

I took my family to another part of the cemetery and showed them the gravestone at Megan's burial plot. It was the first time many of them had seen it. Once again, we cried and we shared our sorrow and joy of being together. I feel that the death of so many people in my life has made me more mindful of the present. I value the present and the time that I am given to be with the people that I love. This was one of those times when I wanted to cherish each moment.

After we left the cemetery we went to the local V.F.W. hall. I wanted to show my family the photo of my father and the plaque commemorating his service during World War II. We continued to the World War II monument in town and looked up his name on the memorial. It was very moving to visit these places with my family, talk about my father's medals from the war, and discuss memories of the family.

We all went back to the house and visited. We had a barbecue for dinner and really started to enjoy our time together. In the evening we sat around in the living room and dining room talking and laughing. It turned into a really nice family time. At one point my niece took a video clip of us on her cell phone. When she played it back to look at it she was disappointed and said that it hadn't come out. She was upset because the video clip was full of some sort of interference. I looked at it and was shocked to see what appeared to be small orbs flying all around us in the video. We started to take turns taping ourselves with various cell phones. The orbs appeared on all of our cell phones! We adjusted the lights and the angles to see if we could debunk whatever it was that we were seeing. The orbs that we saw flying around us kept appearing. In fact, some of them seemed to go behind our heads and show up on the other side. We will never know for sure, but we felt that it might be some spirits of all of our loved-ones' spending time with us.

The next morning, we woke and enjoyed a big country family breakfast with all of the fixings. It was a beautiful autumn day in New England so we went to a fall festival and air show in a neighboring town and then to an orchard for apples and pumpkins. Later that day everyone left to drive up to New Hampshire where they would stay with Darleen for the rest of their vacation.

Joshua, Part 2

When I learned about the family coming up north from Florida for my mother's interment I asked Lisa if she would want to visit with Gary McKinstry. She definitely wanted to do this. I called to make an appointment but was told that he didn't have appointments on the day that they would be here. I explained who I was, and he remembered me. I said that I knew someone who would be here from out of town and that it was very important that they see him. He made an exception and scheduled an appointment with Dave and Lisa. He did not know anything else about them prior to the meeting. They drove down from New Hampshire to my house and I brought them to Gary's home to meet him. The tape that was recorded during the meeting came out poorly, but I tried to understand as much of the reading as I could.

"It's really interesting the energy I am picking up from you two. It's a young energy. It was like, bang! I'm gone. He wasn't supposed to be gone, you know. I have energy that is younger than it should be and it was gone really fast. 'I had so much to do, but I never got to do it. I'm sorry.' It's not like they did anything to anybody, but they are sorry. They shouldn't have passed, you know. It feels like it was freakish and not supposed to be that way. There is a sense of humor and fun. He doesn't mean any harm. By the way, he's dressed normally. Casual and like he's just chillin'. It feels like blunt force trauma; and very fast. I never got home. I want to go home. I have an odd question, why were they not home? In my brain, all I can think is that I want to go home– to get there." Joshua had moved out and had his own apartment at the time of his death.

"Hopefully you have no guilt. Because it's not a guilt thing. This is more my ideas and what I am thinking. He doesn't feel like an adult, but he was an adult. Some of his thoughts are really smart and some are really dumb. Somebody walked away. Like somebody didn't know what to do so they left. I know this is hard to understand, but someone freaked out when he died and didn't know what to do. They didn't help him. I'm on a dark road. I'm traveling, but I don't know where it is going. I don't feel like he drove there, it's like someone gave him a ride. He keeps telling me he's sorry. 'I'm sorry, I'm sorry, I'm sorry. But I don't think I did anything wrong, I just feel sorry.'"

"There is a very strong lady coming through. This energy is an adult. By the way, she had a family. She's in the kitchen and on the phone. This is a phone with a receiver and cord. The kitchen looks small. She's wearing a house dress or duster. She's comfortable. There's no one around so she's comfortable. She's not cooking." We thought this was my mother coming through again. I guess the Wheel of Fortune wasn't on at the time.

"What is the rose thing about? R-O-S-E?" Lisa stated that her father is called Rosy. "That makes sense". Lisa explained that her father, Rosy, was sick at the time. "They aren't ready for him there yet. Your mother is warm over there. She's comfortable. Her stomach was bothering her for a while. She wanted to eat, but she couldn't. Don't feel so bad. It's not about the passing, more about the closure. You're fine, but there is only so much that you can do. She said to chill out and you'll be fine. Don't freak out so much."

Gary looked at Dave and said that he would make a good officer, like a sheriff or policeman. "You're wicked nice, but I could see the kids at the school where you work being afraid to upset you. You're probably just laughing about it."

Lisa said that Josh was 21. Gary spoke of his son who died a year before. "I'm going to tell you something really weird. I think your son kind of came to me before you came here. Somebody was talking about a gun going off and the lady before you didn't know what it was about. She was confused. I think Josh jumped in early. He does not feel suicidal." Lisa said, "It was ruled that way, but we don't know for sure." Gary said, "He. Does. Not. Feel. Suicidal. I don't mean to be rude, but this does not feel like someone that wants to die. We all have bad days, but this does not feel like that. He wasn't trying to get away from anything. This is not about getting away from you or running away, or life sucks that bad. We all have moments, but this just feels like I screwed up. OK?" Lisa said that the police ruled it a suicide, but that we have our theory of what happened. "I'm going to tell you that this feels accidental. This does not feel like suicide, it does not feel like Russian Roulette, it feels like 'I screwed up. It doesn't feel like he planned for this to happen. In his mind, he wasn't doing anything wrong."

He looked at Dave and told him that it felt like he thinks he let you down. "He didn't want to disappoint you. I know you understand far more than he ever would have believed that you did." He said that Lisa has to forgive him, but with Dave it's different. He's more worried about disappointing him.

"You know what's really dumb? He was really smart. But it's like he didn't want to be; he had a stubborn streak. Where's the canal?" Lisa explained that there is a canal near where they live in Florida. "He's near a canal. He's standing by a canal and someone was supposed to go see him, but they never came."

A man came through wearing overalls. Gary described the way that my sister's second husband had died. Lisa admitted that it sounded like her stepfather. Gary said that he wants to say that he's sorry. "He really didn't know what to do. He seemed insensitive because he didn't know what to do with his anger. He was never happy."

"There is a vehicle accident. It's all sort of interconnected with you people. By the way, your son has a wicked funny sense of humor. You know what's really sad is that he never found his passion. He had passions, but he never found the one he could do. It's so weird that he didn't want people to know that he was smart. If he would have survived would he have ever changed and outgrown where he was? Yes. This was not his plan. He really was not a bad guy. He thought drama was following his sister."

"Your mom is talking about her sister." Lisa asked if she is living or dead. Gary said living. "She's worried about her. There's nothing wrong with her, but she's worried about her. It's really weird saying this, but at some point, we all feel alone like everyone is gone. She's worried about her handling it." Lisa said that she knew I was very stressed. Apparently, my sister was concerned about me. It's as if she knew that at this time I was really feeling the depth of sadness from all of the people in my life who had died.

"I think all of the ones who have passed are watching over you. You've got an army around you. Your mom is not telling me anything special. Just Hi and she's happy. She's complaining about her hip, but it was no big deal."

Gary described a place with a barn and a farm with fields. David said it sounded like the house he grew up in. They felt it was his father coming through. He went on to describe David's father and spoke more about the property. His father said not to underestimate Dave.

Then Gary started talking about a girl cousin that was there. (Megan) Gary said, "she had a million things to do and would be going a hundred miles an hour. She would be friendlier to Joshua than he would be to her. I don't mean it in a bad way, just that she would've talked with him, but he just wouldn't know what to say. She was just more sociable than Joshua. Joshua would be more reserved and quiet. You guys have had enough tragedy. They were both too young."

The Spirit Dragonfly Takes Flight!

Toward the end of 2014, I was working at a job that just wasn't working for me. I gave my notice without any other employment lined up. The loss of my mother was really hitting me pretty hard at this time and I really needed to take a break.

I had been making jewelry as a hobby for about twenty years by then. There was something about working on a project that was so beneficial to me. I could lose myself in the work and forget all of my stress for a little while. I know that one of the things people say when you are grieving is, "Take up a hobby." Well, a hobby can help to relieve stress, but it's really not going to cure grief.

I had been told many times through the years that I should sell my jewelry. I had, in fact, sold a few pieces here and there. Friends had asked me to make things for them and I would sell it for the cost of materials plus a couple of dollars for my time. I had even designed and made sets of jewelry for wedding parties on a couple of occasions for brides that I knew.

Now that I was home I knew I had to figure something to do with my time so I wouldn't get bored. I started trying some new techniques for jewelry. I found it to be really rewarding making leather wrap bracelets and started branching out to other pieces made with leather cords, as well.

I approached Steve with the idea that I would like to form a business out of our home. He was totally on board with the idea. This started the process of getting registered as a business with my town and applying for a tax identification number with the state. If I was going to do this, I wanted to do everything up front and legal.

The bedroom that had been Sarah's as she grew up, then Megan's when she was in high school, and then Sarah's again when she moved back home, was now going to be my craft room. Boy, if those walls could talk! I signed up for local craft fairs, an Etsy account, and created a Facebook page for my new business.

I tossed around names for the business, but a couple of ideas kept coming back to me. The reason I was doing this was actually that I needed to deal with my grief and it had become increasingly difficult to maintain employment with the mounting grief I was experiencing. I started to think about this whole long process that I had been experiencing since my father died in 1999.

I examined the things that had helped me to deal with my emotions and my life. My family was a godsend at this time. I don't believe I could have made it this far without Steve by my side. He would tell me that he had been sent to me for a reason and at the right time. He was right. Sarah and Alex were also my loves. Alex helped me to put a brave face on during holidays and special occasions that I might have otherwise wanted to skip entirely. My mother had given me strength and my life a purpose in caring for her. The rest of my family was a source of love and companionship as we all shared so much grief.

There was something else; the signs that I received from my loved ones on the Other side. These signs kept me strong as I opened my mind and my heart to see and feel them. The rainbows that reminded me of Megan and of my sister and the hummingbirds that made me feel my mother's presence were comforts. The thing that really seemed to be the most prevalent sign from the other side was always dragonflies. I thought about the dragonfly pendant Steve bought for me at The Umbrella Factory. That pendant was meant to be made into the necklace with the beads purchased in Provincetown that day I took Megan there. I still feel that she sent it to me so I would know that dragonflies represent her. I would see dragonflies in my yard frequently; sometimes there would be a dozen or more at a time. They would land near me or on me and stay for a long time. I felt that the dragonfly meant Megan was there, and it comforted me immensely. Like the dragonfly poem, the spirit of the dragonfly would try to see and touch the realm that they had left; able to see us, but not able to reveal its true identity. The Spirit Dragonfly.

And with that, I had the name of my new business, my new endeavor. Spirit Dragonfly Beads.

Around this time the person who ran The Next Step support group, Kathy, had an announcement at one of our meetings. A local psychic had agreed to hold a group meeting at Kathy's house for the mothers in our group. The only thing the psychic knew about us was that we had all lost a child. Kathy wanted us to let her know if we would attend the meeting. I knew that I wanted to go. The night of the meeting we gathered at Kathy's home. There were about ten of us in attendance. The psychic, Amy, started to read us. She did not allow tape recording at the meeting, but we could take notes. Everyone was getting a reading and some of them were incredibly accurate.

When she got to me she said that it was a female coming through. She asked me if I was the "crafty" person. I said yes, that I was crafty. She said that the spirit was glad that I had started my business, and was taking it seriously finally. She said, "She was showing me something new that you are doing that looks like this." Amy then made the motions of someone stitching with a needle and thread. She said, "She sees you doing something that looks like sewing, and it's beautiful. You need to create a website and sell it to more people." The incredible part of this is that while making the leather wrap bracelets I use a beading needle and a strong thread to form the bracelets. Megan had never seen me doing this while she was alive. She obviously had seen me doing it since she crossed over. I felt like I had Megan's blessing for my business.

Grief Counseling

I am blessed with wonderful family and a great group of friends in my life. Some of my friends have been in my life for over fifty years! This fact is amazing to some people and unheard of to others. I am very fortunate to have made these friends and to have maintained their friendships throughout my life. I never take their friendship for granted or assume that they will always be there for me and with me. Like any relationship a true friendship takes work. It requires compassion and understanding. Life happens and changes take place. Sometimes events occur that cause people to part their ways or just lose track of each other. Most friendships come into our lives for a period of time and then leave us along the road through life.

When each of my family members died my friends lent support, friendship, and sympathy to help me through that difficult time. Although none of my close friends had lost a child they empathized with my grief and my struggle to maintain and continue.

After my mother died I started to feel like I was experiencing a cumulative grief. Too many of the people I loved had died! I stopped working for a time and found myself unable to move forward. I knew I was in trouble emotionally. I'm sure my mother would have told me to get back to work, but I had no job to go to. None of my family or friends could help me with this. I felt as though I was beginning to experience such deep sadness that I wasn't sure there was a way out of the despair I felt.

I remember one time when I tried to put my feelings into words for my husband. I started to cry. My crying accelerated to the point that he became worried about me. He wasn't sure how to handle this so he helped me to lie down and tried to comfort me. I thought that maybe this is what a "nervous breakdown" feels like. Eventually, I calmed down, but we both knew I was in need of serious help.

I decided that I needed to find grief counseling. I contacted my insurance company to locate a grief counselor in my area. I was given three names of grief counselors. I called each one to schedule an appointment. They each had a reason not to accept me as a patient. One was retiring, another had a full schedule, and the third one was trying to cut back and was not accepting new clients. I searched a little further out of my area, but still, I had no luck finding a counselor. The closest grief counselor I could find was about ninety minutes from my home. I couldn't see spending three hours on the road for a forty-five-minute counseling session.

I had no interest in going back to counseling with someone that didn't understand the grief that I was experiencing. So, I continued to attend The Next Step meetings but felt that I needed more help than they could provide.

One of my friends called me and said that she had a name of a very good grief counselor for me. She gave me the contact information so that I could schedule an appointment with her. I called the counselor and asked about insurance coverage. She explained that she does not file insurance claims, but that I could submit the bill to my insurance for reimbursement. I knew that it wouldn't be covered if I did that. Then she told me that she would see me for just thirty dollars a visit, but I would have to pay cash, out of my pocket. I agreed to go to one initial consult with her at thirty dollars.

I drove to her home and I was very impressed with the palatial grounds. When I walked into her home I was surprised to see museum-quality artwork and sculptures that appeared to be from various locations around the world. Her home looked like a museum! My first thought was that I can't possibly afford to pay her for her services. She took me into a lovely room toward the back of her home. It was filled with books and collectibles. She began telling me that her method of working with clients involved deep meditation.

Now, I am not opposed to meditation. I have actually gone through extensive training in mediation. I experienced a period of hypertension at one point and had undergone a twelve-week meditation and yoga program through the University of Massachusetts Medical Center that was run by a very well-known specialist in the field. I knew how to meditate. I just never seemed to get much benefit from it.

She went on to talk about the importance of finding what my spirit animal was. Now she was starting to lose me. As much as I believe in the spirit world I couldn't bring myself to cross the line to speak with my spirit animal through meditation. She continued telling me stories about her own spirit animal coming to her in public places and speaking to it even if it upset the people around her. At this point, I began wondering if she was schizophrenic. This was definitely not for me. Around then she informed me that the cost of the session was one hundred-eighty dollars! I reminded her that we had agreed on a thirty-dollar fee. She said that she thought I had to agree that she was worth much more. I told her that all I was willing to pay was the agreed upon amount, I wrote her a check and left. I need to mention here that if someone is in contact with their spirit animal, and they find comfort in it, then they should pursue this type of training. I think anything that helps is beneficial and should be explored.

My friend was anxious to hear about my visit with the counselor. When I explained my reasons for not wanting to return she was disappointed. From that time on she kept reminding me that I need to meditate. She had no children and no understanding of my loss. She thought that I should get over it by now and move on. As much as I would try to explain my feelings to her she just couldn't comprehend them or accept them. I started to find this same friend very critical of many aspects of my life. Eventually, I had to reduce my ties with her. It was very difficult to do so, but it was necessary. Being with her and talking with her only intensified my grief and damaged my emotional state.

In grief, we need to take whatever steps are necessary to help ourselves. No two people experience grief the same way. In my work with senior citizens, I have had many conversations about grief. We don't often think about it, but they are a very vulnerable portion of our society. They have often lost parents, siblings, children, and friends. In fact, it's very common to hear them speak of checking the obituaries to see how many of the people that they know have died on any given day. They may joke about this, but it is a serious issue. Most of us can't comprehend living in this manner, and yet our senior family and friends have gotten used to this being a part of their lives.

We are sad when we lose someone; imagine what it is like to live daily waiting to see who is going next. Senior citizens live daily with the knowledge that their own time is limited, as well. The multiple losses accumulate. I learned to screen the elderly for the level of grief they are experiencing. It's important to assess if they are suicidal and if they have considered a suicide plan. If they admit to one, action must be taken to prevent it and to help them deal with their grief and depression. It is a fact that our elderly population has the highest rate of suicide of any age group. This is a serious social problem in this country.

I believe that the circumstances surrounding a death can either diminish the grief or intensify it, also. The tools we have to work through grief and the emotional ability and maturity to utilize those tools will either help us or harm us.

For many people losing a spouse will be the most difficult grief they ever endure. I have spoken with many senior citizens who have lost a spouse. Many of them have managed well to adjust to the change in their life. This doesn't diminish their feelings of loss and loneliness. It only means that they have adapted and had strong coping mechanisms that they were able to utilize.

I remember about six months after one of my aunts had died my uncle was at a social gathering. Another uncle of mine began criticizing him because he had dated a lady that the family knew. She was a very classy lady and they had been friends before both of their spouses had died. My uncle defended himself saying that he had grieved for my aunt when she died and before she died, as she had been ill with cancer for several years. He went on to state that he had loved her, been true to her, and had taken care of her until the day she died. He said that *she* died, *he* did not die, and he had every reason to go on with his life and enjoy the company of another fine lady. I felt so proud of him and applauded his actions.

When my father died I remember my mother saying that they had not had enough time together. They had been married for fifty years, but she wanted more time with him. Now that's love. She managed well, but she became increasingly dependent on me.

I spoke with a man who had lost his wife to a senseless violent act. He expressed that anger was the most difficult part of the grieving process for him. Although I did not feel a strong sense of anger, as I mentioned previously, I can understand his feelings. The way that a person has died has a great deal to do with how we handle it, and how we recover from it. Losing a spouse is a very difficult grieving process. Just the word to describe it is difficult to comprehend as a description of one's self. To go from being a spouse to being widowed has to be a difficult transition.

The process of losing a parent is something we expect to experience, but somehow it still catches us off guard. After all, it is the natural process of life. Parents are expected to die before their children; children should not die before their parents. I remember thinking that someday my parents would die. I knew it in my heart and mind, but still, I could never really visualize it happening. How can we imagine a life without our parents? They have been with us from the very moment of birth. They teach us, feed us, discipline us, protect us, and help us grow every day of our lives. How is it possible to imagine a time when they will not be here and we will be on our own? We are orphans, as they say.

When my father died I had my first taste of true grief, of mourning. I was forty-five years old at the time. I wondered how it feels to someone who is twenty years old or even a child. If I felt such deep grief I couldn't imagine how they must feel. Later in life, I wondered if the answer is similar to the case of a child dying. Does the age really matter? Can we even measure the immeasurable? Somehow, I think it is more difficult for a young child to lose a parent. Children should never have to experience grief such as this.

A physician spoke to me recently about depression. I have migraine headaches that have been severe enough to send me to the hospital and have been under his care for their treatment. He described the process of dealing with the loss of a child as "unresolvable grief". When we grieve for a parent or a spouse, or anyone else, for that matter, we are able to resolve this grief. We can work through it and get through it. When we have grief from losing a child, according to him, we can never resolve it. It has no resolution; there is no end. We carry it for the rest of our life. That is why it is so intense and unrelenting. When he said this to me it made sense. This is why it has been so difficult to work through. I spoke about this at The Next Step meeting. All of the parents present agreed that this made sense. It finally put a label on our grief and validated the way that we feel.

Who Would You be Today?

Megan in 2005.

A fact about losing a child is that you spend the rest of your life wondering. You wonder what your child would be doing now. Would they have a career? Would they be married? Would there be grandchildren that you will never hold, never know? What would they look like as they aged?

A mother in my group who lost an infant under six months old relayed the story of her baby being with other babies. Now the other babies are having birthday parties. As they go through their toddler stages she wonders what her child would be doing now. We can't help ourselves. We always wonder. We miss the growing up our child was supposed to do.

I have had the honor of attending the weddings, bridal showers, and baby showers of my deceased daughter's friends. I say it is an honor because I truly feel that way about the invitations I have received. I have been asked to make jewelry for several brides, in fact. I feel truly happy for them and embrace their day with all of the love I feel for them.

I have to be honest; there is a real downside to attending these functions. I can't help but picture my daughter standing next to the bride as another bridesmaid. I can't help imagining her dancing at the reception. I see her sitting next to the bride-to-be or the mother-to-be. She would be helping every step of the way. Her friends meant the world to her, and they mean the world to me. I see her ghost everywhere I turn at these functions. I feel her there, taking part in the festivities. We sometimes confuse joy with grief. There is a fine line that separates the two emotions. It's bittersweet.

I imagine the same emotions are present even if your child was older when they died. I am sure the eighty-something-year-old grieves just as much when their fifty-something-year-old dies. I imagine they grieve also because they may have lost the person they depended on when they can't take care of themselves any longer. Their caregiver may be gone.

Rosy & Anne

I met my sister's first husband when I was only about four years old. He was always kind to me and felt like a really cool big brother to me. They got married when I was five years old. I remember going to their house for weekends and sometimes school vacations. In the summers my brother and I would go there for three or four weeks at a time. It was always fun to stay with them. Barbara and Rosy had four children; the first one was born when I was just nine years old. I learned how to take care of a baby first hand by changing diapers, feeding them, and bathing them. By the time I was fourteen I would often babysit all four of them. I have always said that I couldn't love them more if they were my own children, and that statement still holds true.

Barbara and Rosy were divorced when I was a freshman in college. I remember feeling like a big part of my family was taken from me, but I know they had their struggles and it was for the best. I lost track of Rosy and didn't hear much from him for a few years. Once their four children started getting older there became occasions when I would see Rosy again, and we reconnected. We had several good discussions about things that had occurred in the family and basically caught up on events. It felt really good to have Rosy back in my life. He and my sister had developed a friendship after so many years so there was less stress involved in having a relationship with him.

After my father died in 1999 Rosy went to visit my mother with his current wife, Anne. Anne was a very sweet lady and always treated everyone in the family with respect. They told my mother that they would always try to help her if she ever needed anything.

My mother never asked for much, but she used to make really large jigsaw puzzles and then she wanted to glue them together and frame them. She asked Rosy to help her. He went to great lengths to get the right glue and finish off the puzzles just right. He even constructed custom-made frames for them. Then he would hang them on the walls for her.

When Rosy called me to ask if I needed any help in 2004, after my brother Eddy died, I was very grateful. I was going through my divorce at the time and felt very much alone and overwhelmed in dealing with everything. I tried to help my mother sort out Eddy's belongings, but I found it to be an incredibly daunting task. Rosy came on the scene and without hesitation helped us to sort everything out and disperse it to the people Eddy had left everything to. I honestly don't know how I could have managed without him. He was the only person who stepped up to the plate to help my mother and me.

Darleen, being his only child living in New England, was able to spend a lot of time with her father and Anne and she developed a very close relationship with them both. She spent many weekends and holidays with them at their home in Rhode Island.

Toward the end of 2014 Rosy was diagnosed with acute myeloid leukemia and told that he might not survive much longer. We were all shocked. I spoke with him several times over the phone, but there always seemed to be a conflict in scheduling whenever we tried to arrange a visit. One of the issues was that he had to go to the hospital every Monday for blood testing and usually needed a blood transfusion. He would feel good for a couple of days after his transfusions, but then get really tired and unable to do much until the following Monday.

There was a question of whether he would benefit from a bone marrow transplant at one time, but after testing many of the family members there was no appropriate donor found. The prognosis was very poor.

In July of 2015, Darleen called to inform me that he was in the hospital in Rhode Island and might not make it out. It was the day of my grandson's eighth birthday party. I went to Alex's party for a little while and then Steve and I drove to Rhode Island to see Rosy and Anne. He had received blood transfusions and was feeling a little better. Well enough to have visitors. We joked and had a great visit. I told Anne to make sure she was getting enough rest and taking care of herself. I told her I was worried about her. I don't think I had ever seen her looking so run down. When it was time to go I hugged her and told her that I loved her. I went to Rosy and hugged him. He held me so close, so tightly. I looked him in the eyes and said, "Rosy, you mean the world to me." He said, "I love you too, Susie." We left and I cried my heart out. I was so afraid that I would never see him again.

I did get to see Rosy and Anne again. They came to our house in September for a short visit. The four of us went out to dinner together. It was a really nice time, one I will never forget. When we said our goodbyes in the parking lot of the restaurant I knew this would be the last time I saw Rosy. I held him tight and told him that I loved him. I didn't say goodbye. I told him that I would see him later. I guess I figured that was the truth; that either in this life or in another life I would see him later.

Darleen called on October second to tell me that Rosy had crossed over. I was grateful that I had had the chance to see him and tell him how I felt. It's an opportunity that I didn't have with so many others. Rosy knew that he was going and he tried to make the most of his last year of life. He had chosen not to plan a funeral. He wanted a direct cremation with no services. He felt that if people couldn't see him and pay respects in life they didn't need to in death. He made a good point.

I have learned the hard way that we need to cherish our loved ones. Tell them we love them. Say the words; be the person you want to be remembered. Send the flowers while they can be enjoyed. Be genuine. "You only live once" is so cliché, but so true.

A Hartford Reading

I learned that John Edward, the nationally known psychic that I used to watch on television, was going to be in Hartford, Connecticut in March of 2016. I was really excited because I had always wanted to see him. I called Darleen and asked if she wanted to go with me. She definitely wanted me to get a ticket for her also.

On March thirteenth we went to Hartford. We got there really early so we could get a good seat. When the gates opened we were the first in line and the first in the room where the reading was being held. As it turned out there were only about fifty people in attendance. We sat in the front row right at the aisle he would be walking up to talk with people. We both had a really good feeling about this.

I know Darleen was hoping her father, Rosy, would come through. I hoped so also, but I would be lying if I didn't admit that I was hoping Megan would come through.

He came out and began connecting with people in the room. Many people received phenomenal readings. He looked straight at me and then at Darleen. He looked like he was about to say something to us and then he went to the back of the room with a reading. This happened several times that afternoon. We swore that he had something to say to us, but he never ended up with a message for us.

He took a break from readings for a little while and opened the room to questions. One of the things he said that impressed me was in reference to finding pennies and other coins. So often people find them and feel they are a sign from a loved one. He said that when you find a coin you should check the date on it. The date may have some connection or reference to a loved one. Try to think about what that connection is.

We left the meeting without a reading. We were both disappointed. On the way home, we talked about the way he kept looking at us like there was something on his mind that he either didn't want to say or felt he shouldn't say. The look on his face seemed sad, or sympathetic. We wondered if he saw that something bad was going to happen. It seemed very odd to both of us.

Two days later, on March fifteenth we were informed that Anne had died! We weren't even aware that she had been ill. Apparently, she had lost a great deal of weight and was very depressed since Rosy died. Darleen and I agreed that she had basically died of a broken heart.

We will never know if John Edward saw something, or in some way sensed it, but we both feel that he may have had some indication of the upcoming death.

Lost Teardrop

It was the summer of 2015 and I still wore my teardrop pendant with Megan's ashes in it almost every day and had been for over eight years by now. It felt like a part of me and my neck felt bare whenever I took it off. Usually, those times were limited to when I showered or swam. I had also been known to take it off on more dressy occasions when I might choose to wear one of my fancier handmade pieces of jewelry.

One day I reached down and realized that it was not around my neck. I couldn't remember having taken it off, but I couldn't find it. I searched everywhere that I could imagine it being, and even places that I couldn't imagine it being. I searched counters, bureaus, drawers, and cupboards. I even checked wastebaskets. My mood went from sure that it would turn up to panic that it was gone. This was part of Megan's being! It held her DNA! It couldn't be gone. Steve started looking and we literally tore the house apart but to no avail. I cried for that pendant. I prayed that it would surface. It was nowhere to be found.

After a few months, I decided to replace it. I searched online for cremation jewelry and found a multitude of pieces available. I finally settled on a lovely pendant with a lily engraved on the front. It looked really classy, and I knew that no one would suspect that it held ashes. I knew from experience that when people learned that my pendant held ashes they either thought that was incredibly beautiful or creepy.

My new pendant came in the mail and I filled it with ashes from the bottom of the silver vase urn. It was beautiful, and I loved it. I figured that I would never see my teardrop pendant again.

April 27, 2016, came around and it was the ninth anniversary! I put a message in a pink balloon and filled it with helium once again. I released it to Megan in Heaven. As it floated away I said out loud,

"Megan, please send me a sign when we go to Bermuda, so that I'll know that you are still here." Steve and I were planning a return cruise to Bermuda in May and I hoped that she would be on the beach with me again.

For the next two weeks, I planned our vacation down to every detail. I planned clothes for each shore excursion and beach day. I planned both formal nights with which dress I would wear, the jewelry and shoes, everything. I packed items and unpacked them as I changed my mind about items I would bring. I was in my closet and drawers at least a hundred times.

The morning finally arrived when we would pack up the car and take off. Our cruise sailed out of Boston, so this would be easy. I started getting ready for the day and went upstairs to take a shower. I opened the top drawer of my bureau to get out fresh underwear. When I opened the drawer, I saw something that shocked me. I froze in my steps. I had opened, taken items out of, and placed items in that drawer at least once or twice a day, every day. But something was very different today. The contents of the drawer had all been pushed forward, toward the back, and to both sides. The middle of the drawer was empty except for my teardrop pendant, on the chain, with the lobster claw clasp connected and closed. I swear that it had not been there all the times that I had looked in that drawer for the nine months that it was missing. I called Steve over to look before I touched anything.

Steve was shocked when he saw the necklace. I told him that was exactly how I found it. I told him that I had asked Megan to send me a sign that she is still around me when I go to Bermuda. I just didn't expect the sign to be sent on the morning that we were leaving!

I know that skeptics would probably say that it had to be there all along. I can't imagine how I wouldn't have seen it in all of that time when it was in a place that I look in, take things out of, and put things into every day.

In September we went to a local country fair that takes place every Labor Day. Darleen came down for the weekend to go with us. She and I walked around looking at all of the craft booths and vendors while Steve was watching a tractor pull. She saw a booth that said they did psychic readings. She wanted to get a reading. I said that I would wait outside because I just didn't feel like having a reading at the time. While she was in there I was approached by a young lady that had been working in the booth. It took me a moment to recognize her. It was Emma, one of the girls that Megan used to babysit. We embraced and talked for a few moments. I couldn't get over how grown up she looked. We spoke about Megan for a moment. I always love it when people speak about her and remember her. It makes me feel so good to know that she is not forgotten.

I told Emma my story about the pendant. When I got to the part about finding it in my top underwear drawer her eyes got very wide and she said, "Oh my God, Megan put it there!" I laughed and said that I believed that was true. Emma went on to tell me that Megan used to tell her, "If you want to hide something so no one will find it, always put it in your underwear drawer. It's the best hiding place." I didn't know whether to laugh or cry, so I did a little of both.

This was such a gift. It validated that Megan had a hand in hiding the pendant; it gave me a chance to talk about her with another person who loved her; I learned about a new memory of her that is treasured by someone. All good things, and all things we as bereaved parents live for.

Darleen came out of her reading by the psychic and looked a little upset. The psychic had told her some messages from Rosy and Ann. The messages concerned some decisions Darleen needed to make that involved her personal life. One interesting thing about it was the way that Rosy made himself known to be present. He showed an image of taking her to a local ice cream stand, named We-Lik-It. Of course, they had never been to that ice cream stand, but it communicated to the psychic the image that Rosy needed to show. Darleen said that when she would go to visit Rosy and Ann they would go out for ice cream. This is how she knew that it was Rosy and Ann who were there. The rest of their messages followed that acknowledgment.

After she came out I told her that I knew the ice cream stand that was referenced, and that it was very popular in our area. The next day Steve and I were riding in the car and we passed the ice cream stand. We were shocked when we saw that it is under new ownership. The name had been changed to "Rosy's Place"!

The Next Step, Part 2

In the beginning of 2016 the ladies who had been facilitating The Next Step for about ten years, decided it was time to step back from the group. They were both winding down to retirement and were ready to let go of it and focus on other things in their lives. We met and discussed the future of our meetings. Most of us were fine with ending the group and maybe just plan a social meeting a couple of times a year.

I questioned if anyone in the group wanted to take it over and continue our meetings. Kathy looked at me and asked, "Do you mean someone like you?" I had already facilitated the group when Kathy and Chris were on vacation and felt comfortable in doing so. I asked if anyone would be willing to co-facilitate it with me. I felt there was a comfort level in knowing that someone could run it if I were ill or had some other plans for an evening when we needed to meet. No one else felt that they could make that commitment. I figured that I would take the reins, but would cancel the meeting if I needed to at any time.

My first challenge was finding a new location for our meetings. Until then we had been meeting in a church basement. I had become aware over the years that several parents were not comfortable meeting in a church that they were not members of. I wanted to find a location that had no religious affiliation with it.

I was very pleased when I was given permission to meet on the campus of a local hospital. I printed out information cards and business cards with information about our group and its new location. These were distributed to several departments in the hospital. I also delivered them to many of the local funeral homes. Some of the funeral directors were extremely receptive to the information. They expressed their frustration in not knowing of resources for parents who have lost children. Likewise, the Social Service department of the hospital was very receptive to the information.

In two months I was ready to hold the first meeting at the hospital. Several of the original members still attend the meetings. Because we have a very fluid relationship with our members we never have the same people in attendance. Some parents might come consistently each month, while others have a more erratic attendance. There are parents who might attend once or twice and feel that they want to continue the process on their own. Others might attend a few times a year, as they feel the need. Whatever a member needs is acceptable; there are no rules to The Next Step.

We are a non-profit group in every sense of the word. We charge no dues, and there is no charge for attending. We don't ask any questions about finances or insurance because there is no bill. Everyone who has lost a child is welcome, regardless of the age of their child. I have also opened the group to grandparents. A grandparent is the closest relationship with a child other than a parent. I have often thought that if something happened to my grandchild I would be as devastated as if I lost another child.

Through the years several parents who have attended lost their child to addiction. It's important to know that this is a true judgement-free area. No matter how they died, when they died, or their age at death, that is still your baby that has passed. The important thing is to get through it. I have heard the stories of children who have gone to rehabilitation and have successfully "cleaned up", only to fall back to their previous habits and eventually die from an overdose. One of these mothers has worked tirelessly toward reform in the treatment and legal issues surrounding drug and alcohol addiction. She also facilitates a support group in another town for parents of children who have died due to addiction. She has become very involved in the legislature that may affect drug laws, as well.

I am reminded of a mother whose daughter had died from suicide. She came to our group for many of the meetings. She spoke about another mother whose daughter had died from cancer. She said, "Your daughter was sick. You did everything you could to make her well.

You brought her to doctors and gave her medications and treatments to make her well, but she got sick again. She died and you couldn't do anything to stop it. My daughter was sick, also. She had an emotional illness. I brought her to doctors and made sure she took her medication, and she got better. But then she got sick again, and she chose to end it. Neither your daughter nor mine was sicker than the other. They both had illnesses that took their lives." I will never forget this profound statement. It puts so many things into perspective. Once again, we cannot measure the immeasurable, and we have no right to judge.

There is only so much that we can do for our children. They reach an age where their lives are in their own hands. Whether they are physically ill, mentally and emotionally ill, develop an addiction to drugs or alcohol, or put themselves in dangerous situations due to poor judgment, it is out of our hands. I can't stress this enough to parents who have lost children. It. Is. Out. Of. Your. Hands. It is not your fault. If you feel guilt or blame, find a way to let it go.

A mother once spoke of losing her infant. I was reminded of my encounter with the man who had lost his young son. I told her of my theory that you cannot measure the immeasurable. That the amount of time she had with her daughter doesn't change her grief. Her daughter's life had value, no matter how long she spent on Earth. She forever changed the life of the people who loved her. Surely, they will look at how fragile life is in a very different way. Every child, whatever their age is important in life, and in death. There is a reason for their existence.

If you have not lost a child, but instead have a relationship with someone who has, please know that it was not their fault. Release the stigma you may be experiencing. Practice being non-judgmental. Trust me, that parent is suffering enough without being judged for their child's actions.

That's what a good support group does. The group is sometimes the only place where a parent can feel they are not being judged. They can feel their true emotions and say the things the rest of the world doesn't comprehend. In a conversation recently with another mother, she expressed that she feels that we are in a different "realm" than the rest of the world. I agreed with her.

We live our lives differently now than we did before, or than others that we know live theirs. We value genuine emotions and problems more than before. We have an altered level of compassion for others. And yet, we have a decreased ability to accept pettiness. When I hear people complain about ridiculous things, petty things, things that don't truly matter, I find that I have a very low tolerance and even lower ability to accept it. The other part of being in another "realm" is that others have no comprehension of what we experience every day. It's almost like there is an invisible wall that separates us.

Many parents experience difficulty maintaining in the workforce as actively as they had, and some can't seem to function at work at all any longer. While others become workaholics out of the necessity to keep busy. We all do what we need to do to maintain emotional survival. Sometimes after working hard for several years, we find that work is not that important any longer. It might result in a reduction in employment hours, a career change, or even early retirement. The energy level just seems to decline after a while. We might have a need to step back a little. I think this is probably the point when we start to accept our loss.

I mentioned earlier that I take the day off from work on Megan's birthday and on the anniversary of her death. Ten years after she died I am still doing that. I believe that I always will. Call them personal days or mental health days, if that makes it seem more respectable. I don't really care what others think about this. It is important to me that I don't need to put myself in the work environment on those two days out of the year. We have discussed this a great deal in The Next Step meetings. Some of us feel differently about it, that staying busy makes it better, easier. I respect any way that a parent gets through those two days of the year and the holidays, because I know they can be the worst days that we have to face.

As The Next Step moves forward I find that we do not have a lot of members. That's alright. New members only mean that a child has died. We never wish that on anyone. I will continue to get our name known to the public, and I will continue to be there if I can help another parent or grandparent.

Cocoa

I started feeling like I wanted another dog. It had been six years since we had to have Snuggles put to sleep, and I really missed having a dog in the house. I was ready, but my husband wasn't so sure about getting a dog. We talked about it a lot. I told him that this would probably be the last dog I have, and I have always wanted another Boston Terrier. He agreed, so we started the process of finding one.

We decided to adopt a rescue dog. Our first attempt was a fair type of event to see dogs that were available for adoption. I had learned there would be at least one Boston Terrier there. We found the booth he was at. He was a very tiny dog, named Tyson. I fell in love immediately. I wanted to take him home with me on the spot. That's when I learned that it doesn't work that way. I had to apply for him and pass certain qualifications. This included reference checks and a home visit. Our references raved about the way we treat dogs, so that was not a problem. The home visit went well and Tyson didn't seem to want to leave. We were informed the next day that he had had another visit to a home with another small dog and they had gotten along extremely well. He was going to their home. I was very disappointed.

We saw several Boston Terriers after that only to be disappointed time and again. We started to feel that adopting a dog might be as difficult as adopting a child, though neither of us had ever been through that process. Finally, I decided to just buy a puppy. I went online to puppy sites to find one in our area. I soon learned that it was nearly impossible to find a Boston Terrier puppy near where we lived.

I found a site that had puppies in New York that was about four hours from our home. I wrote inquiring about one of the puppies. Then I noticed that there was a female chocolate Boston on the same site that was fourteen months old. When I inquired about her I was told that she was being sold because she was too tiny to breed so she was of no use to them any longer. I was very interested. After several lengthy telephone conversations with the breeder, it was decided that we would drive to New York to get her. The breeder wanted to meet us in a parking lot one hour closer to us, which was great because it cut our day by two hours. Now we only needed to drive three hours to get her and three hours back home.

We renamed her Cocoa because of her beautiful chocolate color. When I brought her to the veterinarian for her first check-up I was asked a number of questions. Did I actually see the place she had come from? Did she like to play? Did she even know how to play? No, no, and no. I was asked if she had been kept in a crate, and I said, "Yes". Two vets felt that she had been neglected. She was very tiny for her age because she had not been fed enough. She was also very weak and couldn't go up the steps to our deck well. She had probably been in a crate all of the time and lacked muscle strength.

We started feeding her three meals a day but soon learned that she only wanted and needed two. Dry food was left out in between meals in case she got hungry. We started exercising her more and getting her to run and walk on a regular basis. She learned to play and interact with us and others.

She gained weight and became very strong. She started running up and down the stairs in our home. We fell in love with her fast and hard. She became our little baby girl. Her relationship with Steve was all play and roughhousing. With me, she was gentle and loving. Before long she had us wrapped around her little paw.

I can't express the level of depression and sadness that was lifted from me because of Cocoa. Every single day she has made me laugh. She is love personified. Cocoa seems eternally grateful to us, as well. She was not a rescue dog, but we rescued her anyway. The really big surprise is that she rescued me. She brought me happiness on another level. I know that anytime I feel sad, Cocoa will comfort me. It's no secret that a pet such as a dog or a cat can bring about a significant change in our mental status and decrease depression. One of the mothers in my group even finds comfort from her reptiles.

I am aware that someday I may have to say goodbye to Cocoa, just as I did with other dogs I have loved. I dread the day that happens, but I refuse to let it prevent me from loving this time I have with her. I refuse to let the fear of loss prevent me from enjoying the joy of togetherness. This goes for dogs and people.

One Decade Later

As the year 2017 began, I struggled with the fact that Megan's ten-year anniversary was fast approaching. On one hand, I felt like it had been an impossibly long time since I had spoken with her or hugged her. I missed her so deeply. On the other hand, it still felt like yesterday since we had stood in the kitchen and I had told her to drive slowly; the roads are wet from the rain. I felt like I had to mark the anniversary somehow.

One of her friends contacted me and told me that I should know that she and some of Megan's other friends had kept their promise to me. They continue to talk about her and to keep her memory alive. This same girl has told me that a framed photo of Megan was at their high school class reunion and there was a moment of silence for her and other members of their class who have crossed. I asked her opinion on planning a small reunion on the tenth anniversary to celebrate her life once again. She said that she would attend and she was sure others would, also.

Around this time Sarah contacted me and asked if I wanted to take part in a fundraiser in Megan's memory. Sarah wanted me to have something that would be a positive focus for this, the tenth anniversary year. The student internship program through Planned Parenthood, that meant so much to Megan, had lost most of its funding in recent months. In fact, we learned that there was no longer a student intern at Eastern. We wanted the funds raised to go directly to the internship program.

Sarah and I began a fundraising campaign. We advertised it on our personal Facebook pages and on the page "A Celebration of Megan Kleczka". I attempted to organize an awareness program and raffle at Eastern to earn money for the program, but I encountered multiple roadblocks which prevented me from holding it. However, there were still several donations made which helped to fund the program.

April twenty-seventh approached, and I became more distressed about it. The date stood before me like a huge wall. Once I climbed it I knew I would enter a new decade of being a grieving parent. I felt overwhelmed by this fact. I felt exhausted. I realized that I couldn't think about having a reunion or any type of celebration of her life at this time.

I had recently started a new job and requested the anniversary off. I knew that I still could not work or function on her birthday or anniversary. I was glad when Steve informed me that he had requested the day off from work, also. He didn't want me to be alone on that day. We decided that we would take a ride down to the coast. We went to the beach and I released a pink balloon with a message to Megan. This time I didn't ask for a sign. I asked her to just stay close and let me know she is around. I don't know why I still ask this of her. I know she is here when she needs to be. I know she will always be here when I need her. I see it and feel it all of the time.

As I write this I am planning a small gathering of some of her friends later this summer. It's neither to mark a special day nor is it really intended to remember her. It's to celebrate the path we have all been on; this path of growth and life. I want to meet her friends' spouses and children. I want to think of what might have been and celebrate these young people who have so often given me their love and support. I wish to maintain a relationship with them as they age. I know that they will keep Megan's memory alive, but I truly want my relationship with them to stay alive. I value them and know that they continually give me a glimpse of what might have been.

Megan with some of her close friends from high school.

It's Just Stuff

Around March of 2017, I decided one cold and cloudy day to sort out some of the boxes and bags that had accumulated in our basement. I knew that a lot of the bags contained clothes to be donated. As I sorted through them I came across a lot of my mother's clothes, which could all be donated to charity. I found some of Megan's clothes, a lot of my grandson's baby clothes, and other assorted things. My husband and I sorted things out and collected boxes and bags for charitable donations. It felt great to start cleaning things out and donate them for the benefit of others. I vowed to myself that every week I would spend at least one day, sorting through items for donation. After all, we didn't need this stuff and someone else could benefit from it. Besides, the day would come soon enough when we would need to downsize.

As I sorted through things I came across my mother's belongings. Each item was looked at. Did I want to keep it? Would a family member treasure it? Should I donate it, or give it to charity? Maybe just throw it away? I won't lie, it was tough to decide on some items. I found items from Alex's childhood that would make me chuckle and remember how tiny he once was. I found Sarah's dance recital outfits from her childhood–definitely a keeper.

One of the days I was going through boxes that were on a shelf. I noticed that way in the back there was a plastic box that I couldn't remember placing there. I opened it and immediately was thrown back to the car accident that took Megan's life. It contained items that had been taken from her car the day we went to look at it. I guessed that Steve had put everything there so that I would forget about it and not dwell on it. I looked through her purse and laptop case. Her school books and papers. All of the pages were curled and browned. I realized this was because they had been wet from the rain that must have poured into the car. I touched the papers and imagined my daughter in the car that was split open, rain pouring down on her and all of her belongings, as she lay dying. Everything had pieces of shattered glass in it, the papers, the bags, everything. I felt like I was being transported to the inside of her car at that moment. I felt what it was like right there, right then. I cried. I fell apart. I cried out, "Megan, what am I supposed to do with this?" I wondered do I throw it away? These things she touched; these things that were with her as she died. Finally, I decided to leave them in the box and put it back. How could I do anything else?

How does any parent who has lost a child handle the pieces of their life that are left behind? Almost ten years and I am still finding pieces of her. There are too many remnants of a life cut way too short. A life interrupted.

Around April of 2017 my friend, Jeanne, contacted me and told me that she and her significant other, Paul were going to see my favorite psychic, Gary McKinstry, at an event locally in May. She wondered if I wanted to go with them. Of course, I jumped at the chance and picked up tickets for Steve and I. The event was held on May 19th at the local Italian Club. Jeanne and Paul were hoping that a mutual friend of ours who had just crossed over in March would come through with a message.

As the event neared I felt that Megan wouldn't come through this time. I focused more on my parents and hoped for a message from one of them. Gary began the session explaining that there were no "good" seats and that he would make his way to all of the tables. I did a little quick math in my head and figured that there were about 100 -112 people in attendance. I wondered how many would get a reading. As he moved around the room and leapfrogged from table to table he continued to amaze people with messages from their loved ones. There were two sisters whose other sister came through to inform them that what they had believed all the time was true. She did not commit suicide, as the rumor mill in town had believed. Her death was an accident.

Then there was the frail elder that came through to thank their daughter for all they had done. Most people teared up or completely cried as their messages came through. They nodded in agreement as Gary spoke; acknowledging the messages as fitting their circumstances.

He had made his way to about three-quarters of the tables when he approached our table. Jeanne and Paul sat there, Jeanne's daughter, and two other ladies were in our group, along with Steve and I. He looked at Paul and said that a friend was coming through. He acknowledged that it was our mutual friend who had recently passed. He told Paul that he had to come and see him. He said that he loved Paul and that he has his back, and always will, no matter what. Gary also told Paul that even though he won't be crossing over for a while he has a greeting committee over there that will be there for him when he gets there.

Gary then turned to Jeanes's daughter, who was sitting next to me. He said that the crazy kid was coming through. Jeanne and her daughter couldn't figure who it was so I said that I thought it might be for me. He said that she is a good kid, but has a crazy energy and is funny. She said, "Hello!" He said that she didn't care about money and if she would have won the Powerball she would have given it all away. She valued friendship to its core. That was what mattered to her. He looked at me and told me that she said I was always nice, and she wanted to thank me. Apparently, sometimes I made too much sense. "A lot of times you didn't think anyone was listening, but they were." Gary said, "And then she was gone, way too fast."

Gary said that a lot of the time we think of those who have crossed as angels, but she would rather be remembered as a fairy with wings flying around wearing a frilly dress. What most people don't know is that when Megan was a little girl she would dress up in pretty dresses and put on fairy wings and hold her magic wand and dance all around. She would tell me that someday she wanted to be a fairy. She even had fairy dust. Another thing that this reminded me of was a sign I had purchased from a local country fair. It is carved in wood and has a fairy on it with the word BELIEVE carved in it. I bought it because it reminded me of Megan as a fairy.

Gary went on to say that someone was cleaning recently and found some of her stuff. It was like, "What do I do with this?" She said that it's okay, you can't keep things forever. She would understand if I had to get rid of things. She said not to feel bad, "It's just stuff." He went on to say again that she wasn't a material person. She's sorry she didn't get to say goodbye, and that's probably the toughest part. She said that she had to leave, but that she will always love me.

We all know that we come into this life with nothing and we leave it in the end with nothing. You know the old saying that you can't take it with you. Well, I guess if you die as an infant, a young adult, or a centenarian this is still true. But what about the items we accumulate in our life? The people we leave behind have to sort through the souvenirs, photos, remnants of what we leave behind. What matters, and what doesn't? As I sort through the items that all of my loved ones have left behind I will forever forward be reminded that it is just stuff. Do I need it? Can I use it? Does it have true value to me? Or will it have more value to someone else as a memento or a valuable item? What use is it? Or is it useless?

I am learning to throw away the stuff and clean away the clutter. Maybe this year I will finally open the boxes of old Christmas decorations and exorcise the ghost of Christmas past. The memories will still be with me. The value of memories never lessens, it never ends. That is what we take with us, and it is what we leave behind, and its name is Love.

to get rid of things. She said not to feel bad, "It's just stuff." She went on to say again that she wasn't a material person. She's sorry she didn't get to say goodbye, and that's probably the toughest part. She said that she had to leave, but that she will always love me.

We all know that we come into this life with nothing and we leave it in the end with nothing. You know the old saying that you can't take it with you. Well, I guess if you die as an infant, a young adult, or a centenarian this is still true. But what about the items we accumulate in our life? The people we leave behind have to sort through the souvenirs, photos, remnants of what we leave behind. What matters, and what doesn't? As I sort through the items that all of my loved ones have left behind, I will forever forward be reminded that it is just stuff. Do I need it? Can I use it? Does it have true value to me? Or will it have more value to someone else as a memento or a valuable item? What use is it? Or is it useless?

I am learning to throw away the stuff and clean away the clutter. Maybe this year I will finally open the boxes of old Christmas decorations and exorcise the ghost of Christmas past. The memories will still be with me. The value of memories never lessens, it never ends. That is what we take with us, and it is what we leave behind, and its name is Love.

Part IV

The Dragonfly Spirit Soars

What I Have Learned...

We all live our lives, grow, advance ourselves as we see fit, and learn from our experiences. Some of our experiences are planned, and some really take us by surprise. We might be happy one day and devastated with sadness the very next day. It has been said that we are on this Earth to learn and grow; that once we learn all of the lessons intended for us our time to cross over to the other side will arrive so that we can learn lessons there. If this is true then I guess some of us learn our lessons sooner than others.

We have very little control, and sometimes no control, over many of the events that happen in our lives. We do, however, have control over our reaction to them. We can choose to learn and grow from the things that happen around us. We can be positive and find a way of achieving positive experiences from our lives, or we can wallow in self-pity. We can choose to share our experiences and try to help others, or remain negative and isolated.

I believe that it holds value to think back to your very first memory. Try to evaluate how that memory has affected your life, influenced your choices, and shaped your opinions.

The way that we learn about death as young children will shape our perception of it for the rest of our lives. I have learned that it is alright to tell children about death in a way that they can comprehend and accept. I believe it is also important to only give as much information as they can comprehend, but not enough to overwhelm them. It is okay for them to believe that when we die we go to the ground and then to Heaven. It's also okay to adjust this to whatever cultural or religious belief they are being raised with. They will learn the full truth of death soon enough.

If children believe that they "see" or "feel" the presence of someone that has passed, it's important to try and accept this and let them talk about it. If you don't feel you can accept this, at least allow them an "imaginary friend" or another method to help them to relate to death and accept it. When children get older and begin to learn the truth about death they need to be told the truth and understand that they are loved and supported.

I know people who have said that they will never have children because they have seen others experience the deep sorrow after their children died. I wish they would understand that even though the experience of loss is so devastating, the experience of parenthood far outweighs it. I know that some people would argue with me about that, and that is their right. We are entitled to differing opinions. I just know that I wouldn't trade one moment of time with Megan for anything in the world. In fact, I would trade almost anything for another moment with her.

As people close to us cross over we need to be kind to ourselves. Allow yourself to cry, to mourn, to be in touch with your sadness and accept the process of mourning. Damage can be done to the human psyche if we don't allow these emotions as a vessel to work through our grief.

When we experience anger as part of the grieving process I believe that we should explore that anger deeply. Exactly what are we angry about? Is it simply because they died? Do we have anger toward a person that we feel is responsible for the death? Do we question something that happened or a medical decision that may have caused the death, or one that we thought might prevent the death, but failed? If we examine anger and find the root cause, it gives us a way to deal with it and maybe resolve it. Resolve it if you can and move on.

We need to accept every bit of joy that life brings our way. Treasure each moment. These are very cliché thoughts, but they warrant being said. Without the beauty and love, that life brings us, we only exist. Without the difficult times, we don't appreciate the beauty and love. Give both difficult times and joy your full attention.

Sometimes you have to have faith and just believe in order to find the truth. We often say, "I'll believe it when I see it". I think that sometimes we have to believe in something in order to see it. In my opinion, there are three kinds of people; those who open their hearts and minds to possibilities; those who are skeptical and guarded; and those who close their minds and shut out possibilities. I choose to be open minded. You might surprise yourself and find joy in situations where you might have found distress if you open your heart and mind to the possibilities. This pertains to many different things, such as foods, music, entertainment, and even other cultures and beliefs. It also pertains to psychics. Not everyone is meant to have a reading, and not everyone should. However, if you are curious about it, then why not try? Find a good, reputable psychic and meet with them. You might be surprised by the outcome and the comfort it brings. You will also be surprised at the number of people who are open-minded about psychics.

The most unnatural thing in life is to survive your child. I use the word "survive" loosely. There is a death of your own soul that takes place when your child dies. You search for a way to survive. After Megan was gone for five years I reached a plateau in my grief. A new normal had evolved in my life. I thought this was the best that it would ever get, and it was for quite some time. It truly felt like my level of grief never changed after that. I realized that I was wrong after I passed the ten-year anniversary. I have reached yet another plateau with this grief. I will always grieve for her, but it has taken on a very different feeling. There is yet another new normal in my life. I have found a level of Peace. Embrace these plateaus and "new normals", as you reach them; they are all you have left because certainly, life will never be the same again.

Sometimes things happen that have no explanation. These might include a text message, email, or phone message from someone who has passed. It happens to a lot of people. Open your mind to the physically impossible and let the potential enter your life.

We all find ways to memorialize the ones we love. Sometimes all we need is to have one little memento that we can treasure; sometimes it's just a memory. As far as keeping all of their belongings–let them go, throw them out, give them to someone who can use them, donate them to a charity. Just remember, it's just "stuff", and that's not what matters.

There is definitely strength in numbers. Find a counselor or a support group when you need one. Reach out to family and friends. The best medicine is talking; venting, with someone else who really understands. It might be the lifesaver that you have been looking for.

Speaking of medicine, when we are experiencing great sadness or depression it can be helpful to speak with a physician about medications to relieve depression, anxiety, or insomnia. After all, we all need a little help now and then. Just be cautious about addiction. Medications should help us through a tough period of time, not become a crutch.

They say to take life one day at a time. Well, sometimes you have to take things one minute at a time, one hour at a time, and build up to getting through the days. There will be times later when months and years pass faster than you imagined they would. Time doesn't heal all pain, but it can ease the sting, and provide us the strength we need to carry on. Remember we do not *get over* the grief of losing a loved one; we *get through* it. It will always be there.

Honor yourself. It's okay to be happy. Let yourself smile, laugh, and dance even through your sadness. Sometimes the best way to feel normal again is to do the things that are normal for you. So, get up, dress, shave, eat, and get out of the house. I promise it will get easier more quickly if you do.

It's OK to feel happy. It's also OK if you don't think of your losses sometimes. Don't feel guilty because you relax and enjoy your life. You deserve it, and so do the people around you.

Communicate with others. Remember that half of communication is listening. Listen intently to what others are saying. Try to understand it, and ask for an explanation when you don't. Speak so others can understand you, and make sure they did.

Communicate with yourself. What does this mean? It means to think about your emotions and your actions. Writing is helpful to evaluate the things that you are experiencing. Keep a journal, make a scrapbook, or write letters to yourself or to someone else. Maybe even write a book. Writing this one has helped me to deal with my losses.

It's alright to walk away from toxic relationships. We all have them in our lives. Sometimes we need to end a conversation, a meeting, or even a relationship. Don't feel guilty about your choice. You had a reason for feeling this way. Life is too short to spend it in situations that hurt or upset you.

Accept help from others. When people offer to help you, take them up on it. As difficult as it is, ask for help when you need it. You'll learn that some people want to help, they just don't know what you need or how they can help. Tell them.

Accept that everyone has joy and sorrow in their lives. Yours and mine are not exclusive. Show compassion toward others because you don't always know the burden they are carrying.

Grief is very stressful. Grief and stress cause health problems if you can't learn to control them. It helps to find things that relieve stress in your life. Maybe you like to put on loud music and dance, run, exercise or in some other way slam the stress that is eating at you. Then do it. Maybe you would rather put on soft, gentle music that will relax you. Find out if yoga or meditation may help to relax you. Do you feel like soaking in a hot tub with lavender oil? Then do that. Maybe a craft helps or just reading. Journaling can also be very therapeutic. Close your eyes and take deep breaths in and out while you silently count backward from ten. This is a great relaxer and can be done almost anywhere. It may take different approaches at different times to find out several ways of relieving stress that works for you. Whatever works, as long as you don't harm another person in the process, is fine. Just figure out the things that you respond to. Keep them in the back of your mind as tools to help you cope and relax.

Don't neglect your health, especially in times of stress. Eat a nutritious diet, exercise, and get the rest that you need. When you are stressed you are more likely to get ill from everything from the common cold to cancer and heart disease. Do everything in your power to stay healthy and strong.

I have not said very much about organized religion. That is because, although I was raised Catholic, I never really felt connected to the Catholic Church. I do, however, believe in God. I pray in my own private way. I feel very spiritual. I know many people would tell me that I am wrong in believing that there is any benefit to observing my spirituality in the way that I do. That's alright. I understand their arguments. I just have not found an organized religion that I feel I relate to. I respect their Faith and know that it has a place in many lives. Embrace whatever Faith you have and let it help you through your grief.

I have learned, and I believe, that there is something, life or spiritual existence, that exists after death. Look for the signs. They might surprise you and bring you joy. Don't think that anything is too crazy. Don't think that you are crazy.

Say "I love you." Say it often, loudly, and strongly, and without hesitation. Don't wait! You just might lose your chance. I've learned that our loved ones are together on the other side. They will be there when we cross over. I have had proof that love never dies. It persists even after death. Embrace it.

We need to experience our own Life; good or bad; happy or sad. We need to adapt, change, and grow with it. There is no alternative. We might as well make it the best that we can. For me, the goal since my daughter died has been to find peace, once more. My goal in writing this book has been to help others find peace.

Acknowledgements

This book is a factual account of events that have occurred in my life and especially in the past ten years of my life. My goal in writing this book has been to help others to heal from grief. There is absolutely no ill intent toward anyone or anything mentioned in this book.

I would like to thank my husband, Stephen, the love of my life and my soul mate. Thank you for walking down this road with me. As I said in my wedding vows to you, "When the worst thing that could happen, happened, you were there. You picked me up and you held me up. You gave me a reason to smile and laugh again." You have supported me through more in our time together than I would have ever imagined. I am eternally grateful for your love, respect, and support.

I also want to acknowledge and thank my daughter, Sarah. I think of a few lines from the song *In My Daughter's Eyes*, sung by Martina McBride:

> In my daughter's eyes I can see the future…
> When I'm gone I hope she'll see how happy she made me.
> For I'll be there in my daughter's eyes.

Alex has helped me to smile again, to appreciate Christmas and life in general. I look forward to being a part of his life as he travels along his path. Sarah and Alex, you are my reason to carry on with life. You are the future to me. I love you both to the moon and back.

Thank you to all of my family who have been there through thick and thin; the ones on Earth and the ones who have crossed over. Your support and love have helped me to keep on keeping on.

Thank you to my dear friends, who have laughed, cried, celebrated, and mourned with me. I could never ask for more loving, kind friends.

Thank you to the parents of The Next Step. Just knowing you are there and understand is a godsend. I respect and value each and every one of you.

A special thank you goes out to Gary McKinstry and other reputable psychics. The work they do every day has reached and helped to heal many people.

Thank you to Megan's friends for remaining in my life. It means much more than you will ever know.

Thank you to all of the teachers, guidance counselors, scout leaders, and camp counselors who helped mold my children into the fine young ladies that they became. The world is desperately in need of strong influences for our children.

Last, but certainly not least, I am ever grateful to my dragonfly spirit, my daughter, Megan. You made this book come to life through me. You have reached across from the other side to support and help. You comfort me when nothing else does, and I BELIEVE.

A kiss good-bye

Printed in the United States
By Bookmasters